RETRAINING
AND TRADITION

RETRAINING AND TRADITION

The Skilled Worker in an Era of Change

by

Kenneth Hall and Isobel Miller

London   George Allen & Unwin Ltd
Ruskin House   Museum Street

331.25924
H 177

First published in 1975

© George Allen & Unwin Ltd 1975

ISBN 0 04 658215 0

Printed in Great Britain
in 10 point Times Roman type
by The Aldine Press, Letchworth

Foreword

This book is about people who have undertaken training in government training centres under the Government Vocational Training Scheme. It is the result of two pieces of research which provide, on a basis of solid fact, a quite detailed picture of how trainees have fared as a result of their courses, and of their own and others' attitudes to their training. Adult training of this kind is only now beginning to be offered in Britain on the scale which some other industrialised countries have for some time thought necessary. The results about which Kenneth Hall and Isobel Miller write are therefore of absorbing interest to anyone concerned with this aspect of our industrial life.

On the whole the picture is reassuring. For example more than three-quarters of those trained were in jobs using their newly acquired skill within 5 weeks of leaving a government training centre. Two-thirds of the trainees were in such jobs some 18 months after leaving; and over three-fifths were still there 5 years afterwards. It also emerges that training led on the whole to higher wages, improved chances of promotion, better job security and improved status.

The Training Opportunities Scheme has now taken the place of the Government Vocational Training Scheme, and the responsibility for running it now rests with the Training Services Agency. What lessons are there for the Agency?

I begin with a negative one. This book is about retraining for *men*. Since most of the courses provided in skillcentres (as government training centres are now called) are in skills traditionally regarded as the preserve of men, this is inevitable. But it does show how timely the advent of the Training Opportunities Scheme is, with its widespread use of colleges of further education, the broadening of the range of courses offered and in conse-quence the upsurge in training for women (who now form well over a third of the numbers in training under the scheme).

On the positive side, the research shows that more needs to be done to help older workers taking skillcentre courses. As the authors point out, it is not that older workers cannot successfully be trained; far from it. But they may need a little more help or a little more time if they are to succeed and feel confident of succeeding. The Agency is now developing new kinds of courses which will, it is hoped, be of particular help to older workers.

The research throws interesting light on why the trainees studied decided to undergo training. The predominant reason given was increased security; and the desire for this was even stronger among younger than older men. The research also shows that men who were unable to use their training

7

within a short time of leaving were unlikely to use their new skills at all. Taken together, these indications show the need for proper caution about plans to increase adult training wholesale as a contra-cyclical measure. It will not be easy to persuade people to take training if it does not seem to offer any better prospect of a job; and vigorous efforts are necessary to get people who have trained into jobs using their new skills if the benefits are not to be largely thrown away.

The book is much concerned with the acceptance by industry – employers, trade unions and workpeople themselves – of adult trainees. It is at pains to explain the historical and industrial background, against which it might have been expected that trainees would encounter a good deal of resistance. Of course such resistance does occur, but again the general picture is reasonably reassuring. There are grounds here for hoping that as the Training Opportunities Scheme gathers momentum retraining will become a feature of working life in this country which is not only accepted as normal but regarded as essential.

Incidentally, from the point of view of the Agency it is gratifying how high, on the whole, the quality of training given stood in the eyes of the trainees. It also confirms the feeling that one of the best cures for doubts about the value of the training given in skillcentres is to take people and show them what is going on.

All in all, a book to study and study again. It provides a model of the kind of objective and perceptive work by which the Training Services Agency will need to be guided as it develops its activities.

J. S. CASSELS
Training Services Agency
July 1974

Preface

This book describes two research projects which studied the post-training experience of adult trainees who had undergone a period of training in government training centres. The purpose of the book is to ask questions of a sociological and industrial relations nature as well as to give a factual description of the situation of the trainees. In so doing, it is a study in industrial relations and the sociology of occupations but should also be of interest to personnel managers and others interested in problems of industrial training and manpower development. Readers interested in industrial relations and sociological problems only may wish to omit reading Chapter 2, whilst those who profess a primary interest in industrial training may wish to forgo reading Chapter 10. But as the book is of a piece, neither of these courses is ideal.

The research projects were financed by the Department of Employment; our dealings with that body made us deeply appreciative of the fact that behind the façade of impersonality which civil service departments project to the public there are many good-natured and dedicated men and women. Not all that we write will please them, but we know that they will understand and we are grateful for their assistance.

Over the years we ran up a serious academic debt, and to include the names of all those who helped would need a list long enough to tax the most persevering reader. So to all our colleagues in the Manpower Studies Research Unit of Heriot-Watt University, Edinburgh, who worked on the projects and helped us, our thanks. Equally, we wish to thank the hundreds of men who participated in the project by answering repeated questionnaires, the instructors and managers of the training centres, the managers and shop stewards in industrial firms and many others who helped and encouraged us. Without them, none of this would have been possible.

The book is split into three parts: Part I consists of the Introduction and chapters on the history of manual skills acquisition and on training theory; the second part consists of the data of the first research project which was of a longitudinal nature; and Part III comprises the final chapter of data which gives the position of trainees nearly half a dozen years after they have left the training centre – and brings the book to an end with a review and conclusion.

The authors divided the labour involved in producing the manuscript. Thus Kenneth Hall was responsible for chapters 1, 2, 4, 9, 10 and 12, whilst Isobel Miller wrote chapters 3, 5, 6, 7, 8 and 11. The authors then revised each other's work and the final revision was undertaken by Kenneth Hall in consultation with Bob Fryer of Warwick University, to whom we would wish to acknowledge our thanks. In common with many other authors, we frequently taxed the patience of our publishers.

Both authors worked in industry prior to taking up academic careers, which Isobel Miller gave up in order to become a full-time housewife, at least for the time being. Kenneth Hall served an engineering apprenticeship, which was interrupted by flying service in the RAF, and later worked in design and development, mainly in the motor industry. His apprenticeship has made him aware of some simple facts which may otherwise have escaped him. Thus, it may well be in the national interest to accept retraining, but when one has spent a number of years on low pay in order to become a tradesman, in the hope of obtaining job security and relatively high remuneration, how reasonable is it of society to expect one to forgo those personal advantages (so important to one's family as well as oneself) for the declared good of others or for some abstract concept such as 'the national interest'? To that author such resistance to 'dilution' as does exist, whilst possibly not to be applauded, does make sense and he feels that any trade union officer who does not take such feelings into account when considering the vexing question of whether or not to help promote 'skills dilution' would be failing in his duty. As an academic, uninvolved in the personal aspects of the problem, he does, however, perceive that it is possible to arrange industrial affairs so that dilution can be advantageous to all sectors of industry.

Isobel Miller worked in 'Personnel' for an electronics firm, specialising in recruitment. She, too, is aware of the fact that people are not slow in preaching to others that they ought to forgo restrictive practices – so long as their own restrictive practices are not questioned.

Both realise only too well the significance of the perception of reality on attitudes and behaviour as opposed to the effects of 'objective reality' – hence the emphasis throughout this book on the 'action frame of reference' (see Chapter 1).

KENNETH HALL
ISOBEL MILLER
Autumn 1974

Contents

PART 1

THE SKILLED WORKER
AND HIS TRAINING

Chapter 1

Industrial Change and Industrial Training

SETTING THE SCENE

This is an era of change and nowhere is this change more apparent than in the field of technology. Industries which did not exist at all less than half a century ago are now major producers and employers of labour. Examples of this are almost too numerous to quote, but would certainly include most of the automative industry, the chemical and electronics industries and aeronautical and aerospace technology. And the rate of technological change is accelerating. If the working life of most individuals lasts about fifty years, then an apprenticeship at the commencement of an industrial career as a once-for-all training period makes little sense, and retraining at regular intervals becomes the order of the day.

With technological change comes skills redundancy and with this arises the problem of redeployment and retraining. It has been assessed that over two-thirds of all investment in manufacturing industry at this time is for the sole purpose of reducing, and changing, the labour content of industry. Any resistance here is bound to make this country less competitive; yet men in our society must work in order to feel that they are worthy citizens, so that throwing men permanently out of work rather than retraining them is bound to produce resistance. If one adds to this the fact that the number of unskilled male jobs in manufacturing industry is declining both absolutely and relatively, then not only the retraining of those with redundant skills but also the provision of some measure of training for those with no skills at all becomes essential. Yet our rate of adaptation to the new industrial facts is slow, and in danger of being too slow; too slow not only for industry itself, but also for those employed in industrial undertakings. Ours is a tradition-orientated society and there is much to be said for this; it gives us a sense of stability in an unstable world. When, however, one considers the social consequences of technological change, then our traditions are an encumbrance upon us. Indeed, if our competitors adapt more quickly to such change, then no amount of scientific and technological innovation will compensate for this inertia.

Tradition is the matrix in which apprenticeship, one of the corner-stones of skills definition, is embedded. Ideally, of course, apprenticeship should

15

have skills acquisition as its main emphasis. Even to the casual observer of the industrial scene this is not, however, a complete explanation, for apprenticeships exist in some skills areas where skills themselves are often very rudimentary and frequently rapidly declining, whilst in certain other skills areas no apprenticeships as such exist at all. So tradition is important, yet as a complete explanation it is lacking. Apprenticeship needs also to be viewed in the context of control – at one time control by masters, now control by trade unions. Apprenticeship as an institution has changed much with time, so that the same word has altered its meaning almost completely, as Chapter 2 attempts to demonstrate. The problem of control, then, is central to the whole argument of skills definition. As one recent observer has put it,

'the unionism of skilled men . . . is quite different from the unionism [of semi- and unskilled men]. . . . The skill controls the job and is solidified in the union. . . . Nor are [the skilled man's] skills solely physical ones. The union as the collective controller of these skills creates within the union leaders other skills. In his negotiations with the employer he is able to call upon a variety of subtle arguments as his members have control of the job. A skilled worker has . . . freedom [and] dignity.' [1]

Much will be said elsewhere in this book with regard to our apprentice-ship system, its history and the present situation. It is enough to state that much of our apprenticeship training has left a great deal to be desired when viewed as a mechanism of skills acquisition, and that other skills – be they those of operators at one end of the scale or of managers at the other end – were until relatively recently thought to require little, if any, training at all. This the White Paper *Training for Skills* of 1962 and the Industrial Training Act of 1964, which followed upon the White Paper, were meant to correct. Much has subsequently been achieved in industrial training and in the main due to the impetus created by the oft-maligned industrial training boards. Yet even now, for a variety of reasons – some of which will be discussed later – little is being done by industry to train in any systematic way those who require retraining or who need to obtain a skill for the first time and are beyond the normal age of apprentice-ship. Certainly there are difficulties when one attempts to train adults, yet it has been demonstrated time and again [2] that these difficulties should not make us opt out when it comes to providing adults with skills, for given the right techniques adults can be taught to perform complex tasks. And this is good news for all of us, for it requires only time to age us all.

So in the main until recently skills shortages were left to God and to the youth apprenticeship system. The only systematic training scheme for adults

[1] H. Beynon, *Working for Ford* (Penguin, 1963), p. 187.
[2] As for example by the researchers of London University's Industrial Training Research Unit at Cambridge; an interesting account is to be found in E. Belbin and R. M. Belbin, *Problems in Adult Retraining* (Heinemann, 1972).

requiring a (new) skill in this country is the government training scheme, and about this there exists what almost amounts to a conspiracy of silence. Which is rather strange, for the scheme functions well and the skilled workers put on the labour market by government training centres are in normal times generally readily absorbed, as this book hopes to demonstrate. The data on which this book is based take us only to the early 1970s, but it would appear from discussions with government training centre managers and others that the situation so described had not changed materially by the mid-seventies in terms of placement percentages and the like.

Sadly, some resistance to the integration of 'adult apprentices' into the labour force is, given the social structure of this country, almost inevitable. Craftsmen have inherited the tradition that a youth apprenticeship *does* equip a man for life in a given trade. They have, by and large, not yet accepted the fact that technological changes within a lifetime may make such skills time and again redundant. Given the industrial situation with its conflict of interests, this is not surprising, yet our entry into the European Common Market makes an active labour market policy almost inevitable and in the long run this is bound to have far-reaching effects on our industrial relations system in this most sensitive area.

In the field of manual employment one does not even have to concentrate upon the skilled worker in order to discern resistance to change. An example of how different groups face varying degrees of rationality is demonstrated by the ferment in the docks in the early 1970s. The packing of cargo into containers has reduced the turn-round time of ships in docks and has improved the safety of cargo in transit, but has also had the inevitable corollary of a reduction in the quantity of manual work available in the docks, not least by moving some of the work into the more efficient container depots which are frequently sited inland. Yet predictably the change was resisted, and given our social conditions then, understandably so. The dockers appeared unable to accept that many of their skills were no longer in large demand, and were unwilling to forgo neither their traditional rights, nor their powers to control. Yet paradoxically, if only redeployment following up retraining were to be accepted as commonplace then the convulsions within the docks industry could have been averted. Perhaps, given our industrial situation, such necessary changes will arise only gradually.

THE RESEARCH PROJECTS IN THEIR CONTEXT

We describe here two research projects undertaken by the Manpower Studies Research Unit of Heriot-Watt University in Edinburgh, whose object it was to assess the effectiveness of the government training centres scheme. These projects were not the only ones to be undertaken in this field [3] yet they were relatively unique in a number of ways. Thus the first

[3] The Social Survey Division of the Office of Population Censuses and Surveys carried out a follow-up study of trainees who were on courses in government training centres in 1965. See *Post-Training Careers of Government Training Centre Trainees* (HMSO, 1972).

study was a longitudinal one which monitored the post-training experience of 258 Scottish and 37 English trainees at regular intervals over an eighteen-month period, using rigorous control groups in order to establish that which was unique to these trainees as against that which was commonly experienced by a broad spectrum of industrial workers. The aim of a continuously high response rate was achieved in that contact was maintained with over 97 per cent of trainees – and broadly similar percentages of control groups – over the period of the longitudinal study. The initial interviews with the trainees took place in the training centres in 1968 and 1969, the field work being completed in 1971. Answers were sought to a number of questions as, for example: why mature men volunteer for training, what return they get on their investment, how they cope with the complexities of the post-training situation. In a host of ways these objectives were achieved, yet there still remained one overriding problem which led to a second study being mounted. The monitoring period of eighteen months indicated that some men were achieving full integration into the labour force of skilled men, whilst other groups completely failed to do so and thus abandoned their training trade. A year and a half is too short a period to see the completion of this process. Ideally, then, the study should have been continued, yet this was for practical and economic reasons not possible. Hence the alternative approach for the solution to this problem was accepted, and a study was initiated whose purpose it was to contact as many as possible of the trainees who had left their centre some five or more years earlier. This second group of men had passed through their training centre in 1964 and 1965. The main part of the fieldwork was completed in 1971 and the analysis of the data took us into early 1973. As in the first study, the overriding aim was to establish meaningfully high response rates.

Inevitably, most industrial studies have a regional bias. Thus, for example, Joan Woodward's south-east Essex studies [4] and Goldthorpe *et al.*'s Affluent Worker study, which took place in Luton.[5] And Scotland has been the location of one of the best-known post-war British industrial studies.[6] Yet we were aware that a purely Scottish study could lead to questions as to its utility for Great Britain as a whole. The small English sample of trainees was to verify if this was so or not. In the event it became clear to us that whilst regional differences do exist, they in no way invalidate the findings of this study – a conclusion reinforced by the work of the Social Survey Division,[7] whose findings broadly, where comparable, validated ours.

These studies were fortuitously timed, for 1972 saw a change in the

---

[4] J. Woodward, *Industrial Organisations: Theory and Practice* (Oxford University Press, 1965).

[5] J. H. Goldthorpe *et al.*, *The Affluent Worker: Industrial Attitudes and Behaviour* (Cambridge University Press, 1968).

[6] T. Burns and J. Stalker, *The Management of Innovation* (Tavistock, 1961).

[7] See footnote 3.

Government's policy as it relates to involvement in the labour market, possibly in anticipation of our entry into the Common Market. Until that year the Government had played a relatively passive role. With the United Kingdom unemployment figure exceeding the magic million mark early in that year memories of the social and political unrest of the 1930s were reawakened, and the Government decided for good or ill to play a more active role. Thus February of 1972 saw the publication of the consultative document 'Training for the Future – a Plan for Discussion' following which in August of that year the Training Opportunities Scheme was launched, whose purpose it was to increase government financed training places from 18,400 in 1971 to an intended 100,000 by the end of the decade. This was followed in November by an announcement by the Secretary of State for Employment of his intention to set up a Manpower Services Commission to co-ordinate the employment and training services of his department and in December of 1972 the paper 'Into Action – a Plan for a Modern Employment Service' was published, which promised to modernise the Department of Employment's employment services and to gear them more closely to the requirements of its customers. These intentions were put into effect in 1973 and the Training Services Agency came into being in August of that year. All these are significant innovations, but for the purpose of this book the Training Opportunities Scheme is the most important new enterprise. To comprehend its significance one has to look at the statistics of skills training.

The number of young people entering youth apprenticeships in the early 1970s was some 105,000 boys and about 16,000 girls annually, thus making a grand total of some 121,000 apprentices. About the same number of young people were entering upon a course of training for a variety of other skills not normally assumed to require an apprenticeship. The government training centre situation in 1972 was that there were 52 government training centres providing training in 51 trades. The centres had about 11,000 training places and the output of the centres had been 18,400 trainees in 1971. In the light of the Training Opportunities Scheme these figures are to change dramatically. The plan is that the output is to be raised to between 60,000 and 70,000 by 1975 and to 100,000 as soon as possible thereafter. These targets may themselves have been conservative, as the half-way mark of the intended maximum number had been reached by the end of 1973. Industrial and educational premises in addition to the much extended training centres are to be utilised in order to achieve this target. It will now be patently obvious that when these proposals are fully implemented adult apprentices will, to all intents and purposes, have parity in numbers with youth apprentices. From this it follows that much of the skills requirement of industry is to be met in future from this alternative source. It is with this in mind that this book is written, for the men described here are likely to be prototypical of many of the new generation of men who will graduate into industry via the Training Opportunities Scheme.

In the intervening period before these men arrive on the industrial scene in their vast numbers, the idea of grown men undertaking a course – albeit an accelerated course – akin to an apprenticeship must at first strike one as incongruous. This must be especially so if one has been raised in an industrial environment permeated by the ideology of youth apprenticeships. One could of course put forward a variety of reasons why the acquisition of a high-level manual skill should be the prerogative of youth. Certainly youth apprenticeships were ideally suited to the medieval scene, but over the centuries it has become ever more difficult to reconcile the apprenticeship system with the technological system and one is left to speculate on the relative significance of tradition and of trade union control as important determinants of its unimpeded continuance. This is not of course to suggest that systematic teaching of skills to the young should be abandoned; far from that, for one suggestion worth following is that youth apprenticeships should be overhauled and improved – and shortened to take account of the real skills requirements of the trade rather than the ritualistic requirements of tradition. The constructive work of some training boards – and the co-operation of some trade unions – has already had its effect here. The real proposal could be that such training should not be the monopoly of the young alone. It has to be conceded that youth apprenticeships still have much which is in their favour; for example, skill learning has always been considered to be easier for the young, if only because memory plays an appreciable part in learning and the young have the advantage here. Additionally the young are better able to carry the financial burdens associated with a relatively prolonged training period than are older men who must meet the financial responsibility of a family. Yet even here there is hope for the adult, for the one skill necessary to facilitate learning is to have successful periodic learning increments behind one [8] and this the Training Opportunities Scheme is likely to facilitate as more and more adults are given regular 'doses' of learning over the period of a lifetime. As regards financial problems of adult retraining, these certainly require a solution, yet here again the Training Opportunities Scheme has provided a start by giving at least reasonable grants to adults who are training under the scheme.

During the last decade much has been written, in this country and elsewhere, on the subject of manpower planning. A preliminary analysis of the data from a study at present under way at the Manpower Studies Research Unit of Heriot-Watt University leads one to the tentative conclusion that the large amount of talk here has so far produced relatively little action. Yet it is still generally accepted that manpower forecasting is, or should be, an important tool for economic planners in advanced industrialised countries. It must, however, be patently obvious that difficulties are almost bound to be met at all levels of manpower forecasting – at national and regional levels as well as at the level of the individual firm.

[8] E. Belbin and R. M. Belbin, op. cit.

When these difficulties are added together they are likely to inhibit accuracy in manpower planning. These difficulties emphasise the need for a facility which can relatively quickly rectify miscalculations in the forecasts. The significance here of the government training scheme becomes apparent, for the alternative youth apprenticeship system is for a whole host of reasons unable to provide for the speedy rectification of miscalculations. Yet the difficulties here should not be minimised, for resistance from a variety of industrial quarters should be expected. On the other hand, the common mythology of complete non-acceptance of non-apprenticed men into the company of the skilled does not stand up to analysis, as we hope to demonstrate later. It is not argued that non-acceptance is not understandable – indeed for employers, trade unions and skilled workers non-acceptance may for a variety of reasons be wholly understandable – but merely that it has been commonly exaggerated, and the majority of the trainees described in this book managed to overcome resistance from whatever quarter, when met.

Given the high rate of success of government trainees – some two-thirds of all our main group trainees were in 'skilled jobs' some eighteen months after leaving their training centres and 60.2 per cent of the other group were still there more than five years after completing their training – one is left with the problem of the 'drop-outs'. Given the 'ethic of success', why did some men not pursue their new career with more vigour? This question is only partly answered in later chapters.

THE PROBLEMS OF RETRAINING

Obviously, retraining has advantages and disadvantages, depending very much on one's own industrial situation. Yet we would argue that on balance the advantages greatly outweigh the disadvantages.

To those who run the economy, the advantages must be obvious – the first necessity is to have a smooth-running economy. This explains the increase of government intervention in the labour market which appears to be moving us inexorably towards the Swedish labour market model with its policy of very active government intervention indeed.

Equally, managements have problems which are likely to make some of them inclined to support adult retraining – though surprisingly we did find evidence of management resistance of not insignificant proportions to the 'dilution' of the skilled labour force by adult trainees. In industries which have and are enjoying rapid expansion as, for example, chemical and electronics, the supply of skilled men is likely to be short of demand and here managerial support could be expected. Managers who want organisational and technological change are likely to require flexibility, which may make some of them support the concept of retraining. To managers in declining industries, however, unless they intend to haul themselves out of the rut, the problem of retraining – except as a mechanism of ridding themselves of surplus labour – is not likely to be of much interest.

The problems of redundant and unemployed persons who do not possess skills in demand are obvious – they require a mechanism which will get them quickly and smoothly back into the labour force. Yet at least some unemployed who were eligible for retraining refused the opportunity when offered, and our control group of unemployed – see the chapter on methodology – were of this ilk.

The problems of school-leavers are of a different nature: as retraining of adults becomes more commonplace, they may find it more difficult to obtain apprenticeships. Given the assumption that apprenticeship skills have consequences in the fields of status, job security and autonomy, the problems of young people endeavouring to obtain an apprenticeship should not be minimised.

Then there are the problems which those trade unions which organise skilled men face. The dilemma of such unions in an era of union amalgamation and the growth of general and industrial unionism cannot be ignored. Some of these problems are discussed in Chapter 9.

When one groups all these problems together, they can be seen as problems of conflict and policy. And that is what this book is really about: how individuals who have gone through the retraining process cope with the difficulties which such problems engender. Inevitably to suggest that time-served men accept 'dilutees' (i.e. men who have not served a full apprenticeship yet wish to be classed as craftsmen) is bound to lead to conflict – how could it be otherwise? Here, as so often elsewhere, one man's solution to his problem is the other man's problem. Possibly one of the surprising results which stands out clearly from our research (see Chapter 9) is the high measure of real generosity shown by so many craftsmen. It behoves our policy-makers to channel this generosity and under no circumstances to alienate those who have acquired their skills in the traditional manner.

We did gain a little insight into the process of government policy decision-making, but far too little to be of much use in allowing us to understand the process clearly. And whilst we attempted to gauge managerial attitudes to retraining (see Chapter 9), this was too cursory to be of great utility. Thus finally we were by finances, time and circumstances forced to focus our main attention on only one aspect of the complex situation: that of the trainees in the labour market attempting to compete with men trained via the more orthodox channels of a youth apprenticeship.

The purpose of this book, then, is to describe and explain what happened to two groups of government trainees, in order to gain an insight into the difficulties which individuals and, to a lesser extent, industrial firms are likely to meet when the large numbers of new trainees come on to the labour market. Following the first four introductory chapters, Chapters 5 to 10 inclusive are related to the 'longitudinal' study, whilst Chapter 11 describes aspects of the five-year follow-up project.

Seen from the trainees' point of view, retraining may be perceived as an investment which the individual makes in himself, in clear anticipation of certain objective consequences. Following Lockwood, it is useful to understand the social consequences of employment and unemployment in terms of market, work and status situations.[9]

MARKET, WORK AND STATUS SITUATIONS

The market situation deals with such issues as wages, hours of work, holidays, security, chance of promotion, probability of pensions and so on. Now, clearly most of our trainees hoped for – and to some extent realised – gain in some or all of these areas. We discuss especially wages and the search for security in some detail later, and other market issues in passing. It is hardly surprising that those of our trainees who managed to gain a secure foothold in skilled work almost invariably improved their market situation. In the words of a recent commentator, 'as Max Weber indicated, the possession of a recognised skill . . . is the major factor influencing market capacity'.[10]

The work situation covers a whole host of issues, such as tightness versus lack of supervision and personal autonomy, and is based on the organisation of production. Whilst it is difficult to generalise, it would not be unreasonable to state that skilled manual workers in a variety of industries do possess a high degree of personal autonomy in their work, and make decisions which are made for less skilled workers by management.

The work situation leads us back to another aspect of control: the skilled worker is frequently much more in control of his working life than his less skilled counterpart. As Beynon put it,[11] 'in a society where most people have only their labour power to sell, a conflict over control will be a feature of work situations'. Yet it would be ludicrous to suggest that all persons who have only their labour power to sell are of a homogeneous nature. Indeed, the same author, in describing a discussion on a job evaluation grading exercise with a shop steward, states that 'throughout the evening [the steward] argued that the grading agreement was an attack on the skilled worker who had for too long benefited at the expense of the semi- and unskilled'.[12] Whilst this discussion presumably referred to the market situation of skilled workers, the fact that the work situation of the line worker in a car-assembly plant differs so markedly from that of the skilled man – the one being ground almost into insensibility by the routinised nature of his work, whilst the other often possesses a fair measure of power to decide how and even when to do a certain job – was bound to be in the steward's mind.

Throughout the book, the reader will note references to the change in the work situation which the trainees expected, and whilst we concentrated

[9] D. Lockwood, *The Blackcoated Worker* (Allen & Unwin, 1958).
[10] A. Giddens, *The Class Structure of the Advanced Societies* (Hutchinson, 1973), p. 103.
[11] H. Beynon, op. cit., p. 129.
[12] *ibid.*, p. 167.

more on the market than the work situation, taking the second possibly too much for granted, we were struck by the many comments which made it clear that trainees were not unaware of their improved work situation upon successfully obtaining and holding skilled jobs. The status situation deals with the problem of prestige. It goes almost without saying that skilled work carries in our society a significant measure of prestige and hence of social status. Thus when Martin asked people what jobs they would like their sons to take up, it was professional and skilled manual tasks which came out on top.[13] There is a clear tie between economic position and social status, and further that 'economic advantage does not simply confer social status; in many cases traditional social status is a ground for the perpetuation of economic differences'.[14] Much will be said in later chapters of the class and status situation of men who require a skill in later life; here it can be said that whilst for many trainees not as significant as the market situation and for some not as significant as the work situation, the search for higher status was nonetheless a motivator for the search for a skill and a skilled job for many trainees.

THE ACTION FRAME OF REFERENCE AS AN ANALYTICAL TOOL

Much of that which is described on the following pages makes sense only when perceived through the eyes of the participant. The search for a new skill *may* at the end only bring illusory benefits, the resistance to 'skills dilution' may make little sense to the casual observer but may be wholly rational to the participant. It is for this purpose that in more recent years industrial sociology and social theory have rediscovered the 'action frame of reference'. It may be useful to quote from a major industrial study where this frame of reference proved its utility. The authors wrote:

'[the action frame of reference is] a frame of reference within which the actors' own definition of the situations in which they are engaged is taken as an initial basis for the explanation of their social behaviour and relationships. In contrast with approaches which begin with some general and normative psychology (or philosophy) of individual needs in work, or with some conception of the "needs" of the efficiently operating industrial enterprise, an action frame of reference would direct attention systematically to the *variety of meanings* [authors' italics] which work may have for industrial employees. And this in turn would then compel recognition of the fact that in modern society the members of the industrial labour force form a highly differentiated collectivity. . . .'[15]

What then is the basic assumption of this approach? We assume here that the basic assumption is simply that people have differing perceptions

---

[13] F. M. Martin, 'Some Subjective Aspects of Social Stratification', *Social Mobility in Britain*, D. V. Glass (ed.) (Routledge, 1954), p. 69.

[14] D. Lockwood, op. cit., p. 100.

[15] J. H. Goldthorpe, *et al.*, op. cit., p. 184.

of social reality and to people it is these perceptions rather than the reality itself which is meaningful and in turn produces responses. Industrial life is heavily laced with conflict – given the differing perspectives of industrial life held by the various major groupings this is hardly surprising. When one deals with an area of the industrial world so complex as that which seeks to change the definition of who shall be entitled to the term 'craftsman' and who shall not, conflict is almost inevitable.

Throughout the studies which the following pages describe, we have attempted to describe not only the objective facts, even though these have been paramount in our minds, but also the meaning which the various groups and their members assigned to them. In so far as we have done so, an 'action frame of reference' has been utilised.

Inevitably, authors of books which are based on research hope that their work will be meaningful to a host of interested readers. In this the authors of this book are not unique, for having spent much of one's work and 'leisure' over a period of time pursuing a piece of research, one naturally hopes that this will have served a useful purpose. . . . Inevitably also, no matter how much one aims for scientific detachment, one gets involved in the human problems of one's subjects. The trainees who are the subject of these studies remained loyal – a process which must on occasions have been difficult – and they have our gratitude. These men were attempting to enter a 'club' to which membership is normally gained by 'serving one's time' in a youth apprenticeship and had not been indoctrinated into the 'mysteries' of the trade in the more usual way, which for some led to difficulties in adjusting to the role of craftsman. The established craftsmen too deserve sympathy; they have the shattering experience of frequently seeing their work competently performed by men who have not served an orthodox apprenticeship and who are looked upon as 'six-month wonders' thereby threatening their status and much else. It says something for such men's tolerance that the story revealed on the following pages is one indicating a fair measure of success for the new adult apprentice system. The cathartic effect of the next ten years, as the trainees enter the labour market in ever-growing numbers, is left to the reader's imagination. Yet paradoxically in the final analysis it could be to everyone's advantage if the process of changing tradition in this tradition-bound corner of industrial life were accomplished. Then the craftsman whose skill becomes redundant need not defend it beyond the point of utility – he has merely to offer himself for retraining in a new skill which is in demand. So tolerance may bring its own reward.

Chapter 2

Apprenticeship History

THE MEANING OF 'APPRENTICESHIP'

To this day it is a common assumption that only persons who have served a bona fide apprenticeship are capable of undertaking certain types of skilled work. Others who attempt to do so are variously labelled as 'amateurs', 'dilutees' and by other similar terms of deprecation. Yet the mystique which surrounds a craft skill is by no means unique; professions use similar techniques to keep out the uninitiated. For example, the term 'quack' is applied to a person attempting to practise medicine who has not acquired his skill through the orthodox channels. But to the acquisition of a craft skill in this country an additional barrier has been erected: that of age limits for the commencement of the training period. There are historical and practical reasons as to why this should be so, yet the reasonableness of this state of affairs for society as a whole needs to be questioned; for practitioners the advantages are obvious. If the age barrier is now a hindrance to economic growth then it may be in order for society to seek changes – always provided that thereby social injustice is not perpetrated against those who by previous sacrifice already possess a craft skill. The Industrial Training Act of 1964 with its predecessors, the Carr Committee's Report [1] and the White Paper of 1962,[2] to say nothing of the activities of many of the industrial training boards now in operation, are clear indicators that the concept of youth apprenticeships is very deeply ingrained indeed in our industrial culture. What, then, is an apprenticeship?

The *Concise Oxford Dictionary* defines an apprentice as 'a learner of a craft, bound by service, and entitled to instruction from his employer for a specified term'. Apprenticeship is a contractual relationship and, in this country at least, the State accepts the contractual nature of the agreement. The courts will certainly accept that, if an employer terminates an apprenticeship without good cause, e.g. misconduct, then the apprentice is entitled to damages for breach of contract, but the courts do not define

[1] *Training for Skill – Recruitment and Training of Young Workers in Industry* (HMSO, 1958).
[2] Ministry of Labour, *Industrial Training: Government Proposals*, Cmnd 1892 (HMSO, 1962).

26

the content of the contract. The validity of the apprenticeship is based on the completion of the 'specified term' of the contract and not on the 'instruction' to be given. Nor has this situation changed materially with the arrival on the scene of the industrial training boards established under the Industrial Training Act to supervise the training within specific industries, for they can only withhold grants from employers who do not conform to their boards' standards, and when the grant-levy powers of the various boards are in due course removed, as is the present intention, then even this power will have disappeared. Even now the boards do not possess the power to force employers to adhere to the set standards.

Despite modern legislation the general situation has not changed materially since the days of the abolition of the Statute of Artificers. More than forty years ago a government inspired report [3] defined apprenticeships in words not at all dissimilar to those of the Oxford Dictionary, by stating, 'Apprenticeship is the contractual relationship between an employer and a worker under which the employer is obliged to teach the worker . . . and . . . the worker is to serve the employer . . . on stated terms.' This is still the case today, so far as the contractual relationship goes. Yet if the foregoing suggests that the contractual relationship is limited to two parties only, then this is a gross oversimplification. The situation is that 'the apprenticeship system . . . has a third element, the function of regulating entry into a skilled occupation, and it involves trade unions as a third party. Hence, also, the individual apprenticeship contains a third element, namely the provision of admission into a protected trade'.[4] The first two elements of apprenticeship referred to are of course the reciprocal obligations between an employer and his apprentice.

A number of pertinent questions regarding apprenticeship *per se* could be asked; one could for example question the quality of the training given during the period of the indenture. The whole history of the fifties which preceded the Industrial Training Act indicates that serious questions about this were then being asked.[5] But possibly the most relevant question to ask relates to the very existence of apprenticeships: how did the situation as it now is arise at all? This requires us to trace the origins of the system and its subsequent history.

The history of apprenticeships goes back almost into the early times of civilised man, to the Babylon of 2250 BC and the Code of Hammurabi. It is not proposed to relate this early history, for 'the traditions of apprenticeship were inherited from guild regulation and statutory enforcement, but by the middle of the nineteenth century these supports had long been withdrawn and the system survived through custom maintained by the craftsmen and acquiesced in by the employers'.[6]

---

[3] Ministry of Labour, *Report on an Enquiry into Apprenticeship and Training for Skilled Occupations in Great Britain and N. Ireland, 1925–26*, VII (HMSO, 1928), p. 8.
[4] K. Liepmann, *Apprenticeship* (Routledge, 1960), p. 14.
[5] See for example G. Williams, *Recruitment to Skilled Trades* (Routledge, 1957).
[6] H. A. Clegg, A. Fox and A. F. Thomson, *A History of British Trade Unions since 1889*. Vol. 1 (Clarendon Press, 1964), p. 5.

It is proposed to commence this analysis with the history of the medieval craft guilds in so far as they affected the training of apprentices and the definition of who shall be accepted as a craftsman. Although the major part of the research project to be described in this book took place in Scotland, the emphasis will be placed on British economic and social history. There are good reasons for doing so; if there were any differences within the British Isles, then it has been suggested that there was, over most of the period under consideration, a greater difference between northern England and southern England than between the Scottish Lowlands and northern England.[7] Especially after the Act of Union, working-class experience in the industrial parts of Scotland, as well as in England and Wales, produced attitudes which as an amalgam affect industrial relations in all parts of Britain to this day.

THE EARLY DAYS

In Britain, after about AD 1100, production in towns by freemen developed. The craftsman of the day owned his own capital – shop, tools, materials – and such labour as he used was drawn mainly from his own family, although outside help was sometimes called upon. His customers would have been consumers, merchants or other craftsmen who finished the product.[8] Most medieval products were supplied to the local market; yet gradually the growth of towns gave rise to specialisation. The medieval town was, throughout western Europe, very small by modern standards (in Britain only London could boast a population much in excess of 5,000), but, despite this, great diversity of occupations was to be found in the towns: trade, manufacture, craftsmen, servants.[9] The merchants because of their wealth almost invariably became the most powerful group. Quite naturally these merchants wished to protect their wealth and power, and did so by forming in each town trade associations. First to arrive on the scene, then, were the so-called 'guild merchants', some of whom were to be found shortly after the Norman Conquest. Merchant guilds comprised all the sellers of the town, and possessed a statutorily safeguarded monopoly.

Craft guilds soon followed the guild merchants and became important in the thirteenth and fourteenth centuries. In the later Middle Ages each town possessed a wide range of craft guilds which covered the principal trades of the town. A craft guild could comprise one type of seller, e.g. fishmonger, or one type of manufacturer, e.g. armourer.

Our interest in guild merchants is strictly limited; they were first off the mark and as such set the course which other guilds were to follow. The regulations governing entry into guild membership are a case in point; it

---

[7] I. F. Grant, *The Social and Economic Development of Scotland* (Oliver & Boyd, 1930).

[8] G. Clough and C. D. H. Cole, *An Economic History of Europe* (Heath, 1950), Chapter 2.

[9] M. W. Flinn, *An Economic and Social History of Britain* (Macmillan, 1965).

was not easily obtained and in general there were only three ways of securing such entry: by patrimony (father introducing his son into membership); redemption (payment of a heavy fine); and apprenticeship. By the fourteenth century craft guilds had virtually replaced the more general guild merchants.

In the early days of the craft guilds, masters, apprentices and journeymen saw themselves as belonging to a greater or lesser extent to the same social class, and society at large adhered to a similar view. 'They were a proud fraternity, the skilled men of the trade. Their guild represented their common interest [and] managed the affairs of the craft within the town . . . to the general satisfaction of masters and men.' [10] Such harmony is not to be found in industry today; even when modern industrial relations are seen by workers in harmonistic terms [11] the two sides of industry are still clearly defined; yet the guild situation in its early stages claimed nearly absolute harmony. The reason for this was that the apprentice could safely look forward to becoming a master in due course.

Yet gradually all this changed; as time progressed the master became less of the brother craftsman and more of the entrepreneurial employer. Some apprentices did still become masters – marrying the master's daughter was one avenue open to the apprentice, who was being raised in his master's family circle. For the majority of apprentices, however, there was little chance of rising above the status of journeyman. In the early Middle Ages, few masters had employed at most more than a handful of journeymen, and most journeymen had then the real prospect of becoming in due course masters in their own right. Now the increasing scale of industrial enterprise was eroding this situation. The early craft guilds had been harmonious organisations due to two basic reasons: the identity of interest of its members; and the latent social equality between the various sides of enterprise. Later on there came distinction between employer and employed, and with it came problems of industrial relations.

In order to restrict competition within trades, craft guilds exercised rigid control over entry, which is where apprenticeship comes in. Apprenticeship did two things: firstly it ensured that a thorough training was given to the future craft practitioner; and secondly it provided a cheap source of labour. We are told, [12] 'there is no need to be sentimental about guilds . . . they were often employers' rings. Apprentices supplied these oligarchies with cheap and docile labour'. This was certainly true during the later stages of guild history and yet, throughout, 'apprenticeship was an education and initiation into the mystery of the craft'.[13]

Apprenticeships varied from five to ten years in duration, the commonest period being seven years. The apprentice was 'bound' by a contract

[10] G. M. Trevelyan, *English Social History* (Longmans Green, 1942), p. 38.
[11] See for example J. H. Goldthorpe *et al.*, *The Affluent Worker – Industrial Attitudes and Behaviour* (Cambridge University Press, 1968).
[12] C. Hill, *Reformation to Industrial Revolution* (Weidenfeld & Nicolson, 1956), p. 71
[13] M. W. Flinn, op. cit., p. 32.

signed by the master on the one hand and by the apprentice or his father on the other. Throughout the apprenticeship period the boy lived with his master who was responsible for the boy's food and clothing in addition to his training. At the commencement of the period a cash payment was normally made by the parent to the master; this was viewed as an investment, for when patrimony or redemption were not available, it was the only alternative available for opening the prospects of a future career.

The later history of craft guilds in the years which preceded the Statute of Artificers saw the distinction between employers and employed and it is hardly surprising that there were to be found in the towns by the fourteenth century

'not only occasional strikes for higher wages inside the guild, but in some cases the formation of permanent "Yeomen Guilds" to champion the interests of the employees and perform the fighting functions of a modern Trade Union. In some trades and in some towns these Yeomen Guilds also included small master craftsmen . . . [for] traders and manual workers were in some trades beginning to separate, and the trader was assuming control of the industry, by his command of the Craft Guild or the Livery Company.' [14]

Yet this movement was not uniform in time and place. In general, the early guilds formed by journeymen were mainly concerned with such matters as small insurance schemes; with time, these guilds widened their interest and concerned themselves with such 'trade union' matters as wages and hours of labour. So industrial relations problems and workers' unionisation – no matter what name is given to this movement – grew, and apprenticeship was one common factor. Apprenticeship meant of course youth apprenticeship; the most common age for the commencement of apprenticeships was somewhere between thirteen and fifteen years. There were good reasons for starting an apprenticeship at such an early age, the most obvious one being that apprenticeships were long and yet had to be completely before the financial commitments of married life were undertaken. The financial limitations imposed on apprentice earnings are to this day a disincentive to adult apprenticeships.

In theory at least the apprentice could, on completion of his period of indenture, marry and become master in his own right; yet the reality was that as the Middle Ages progressed ever fewer had a sufficient supply of capital in order to do so. The consequence of this was that the majority had to find a master and to work for him for a wage; this wage was often paid by the day – hence the name 'journeyman', a corruption of the French word *journée* meaning 'day', i.e. a day labourer. Journeymanship had in earlier times been mainly a transitional stage; it now became a permanent situation for the majority.

The journeyman had an additional disability, in that he could not

[14] G. M. Trevelyan, op. cit., p. 39.

become a full member of his craft guild. This is not to imply that craft guilds declined – indeed there were more guilds with more members in the sixteenth century than ever before.[15] The most important and useful aspect of a guild's function, however, that of cementing a community of craftsmen, was by then largely a thing of the past. Now only masters could become full members of craft guilds, with powers to elect or become officials and to assist with the making of guild regulations. By the sixteenth century the masters had clearly emerged as a class by recruiting new members to their ranks largely from amongst their own kin and from amongst those wealthy enough to buy their way in.

As we have seen, guild apprenticeship started off as a means of giving the requisite skills to the future master craftsmen, and whilst it continued to do so throughout its history, its major effort changed to the training of journeymen. And as time progressed the gap between the industrial haves and have-nots increased.

It is hardly surprising that with the growth of national over sectional power, the State should take an interest in the training of craftsmen – especially if the State's power depends to no mean extent on the economic performance of the nation. This was the situation when the Statute of Artificers came into being in 1563. The Statute was a landmark in the history of apprenticeships. It may be too simple a view to state that until the advent of the 1964 Act the Statute of Artificers was the only major piece of legislation which embraced the systems of skills acquisition and placed them in a legal framework. The comparison between the Statute and the Industrial Training Act is spurious; the 1563 Act was absolutely explicit but excluded much, whilst the 1964 Act left much more of the decision-making rights to individual firms, yet included the whole gamut of a much more complex industrial manpower situation. Yet the 1563 Statute was a landmark; it was an extension of guild regulation to the whole nation under the English crown. For example, 'it prohibited entry to the weaving industry to any who had not undergone a seven-year apprenticeship, and limited apprenticeship to the sons of gentlemen and freeholders owning more land than £3 per annum. It thus closed the industry, on paper at least, to three-quarters of the rural population'.[16] The Statute, then, was no great instrument of social justice, but rather one which gave monopolistic skills rights to that section of the community which *de facto* already possessed such rights. Yet it was not without merit; it enacted that every craftsman had to serve a seven-year apprenticeship under a master who was responsible for the apprentice. Trevelyan [17] maintains that the object of the Act was as much social and educational as it was economic. And the Justices of the Peace, who under the Statute were responsible for the granting of the indenture, were able to interfere if they felt it their duty to do so. Apprenticeships did on the whole work well, for the master had to meet his

---

[15] M. W. Flinn, op. cit., p. 83.
[16] C. Hill, op. cit., p. 71.
[17] G. M. Trevelyan, op. cit., p. 191.

apprentice across the dining table as well as the work bench and such a social connection was bound to make the majority of masters want to meet their commitments in full. The scheme saw many changes which continually eroded its usefulness; it did, however, continue into the nineteenth century, when the Industrial Revolution finally destroyed it only to substitute the *laissez faire* chaos which was not to the benefit of the uncared-for youth.

From time to time attempts were made to modernise the Statute. Thus in 1604 the Commons attempted unsuccessfully to repeal those clauses which restricted apprenticeship to 'sons of sixty-shilling freeholders'. The age was not one of egalitarianism or of social justice; for example, the JPs were supposed to enforce the Statute, but they were often of the merchant class themselves. So the Statute of Artificers was a piece of legislation which accepted the social divisions of its day. In Sir John Clapham's words [18] 'legislators still thought of all people who had no property as semiservile so that entry into skilled occupations was preserved for the benefit of gentlemen and others of living (who then) might have some means to . . . place their younger sons . . . in a reasonable countenance and calling'. For the less fortunate members of society there was compulsion for semiskilled labourers or those labouring on the land. Of job mobility there was little or none; a memorandum issued ten years after the passing of the Statute held that it was right that children should not be permitted to depart from their parent's occupation. Occupational and social mobility were not accepted in the sixteenth century.

Even in periods of history renowned for their lack of change, gradual changes do take place. The interpretation of the Statute by JPs, the exclusion from the working of the Statute of 'new' industries, all this conspired to cause changes, though by no means all of them beneficial to the 'lower orders' of society. Gradually Parliament and the judiciary had ceased to enforce the Elizabethan machinery of industrial regulation. In 1694 the clause in the Statute of Artificers which excluded sons of poor freeholders from the clothing industry was repealed. All apprenticeship regulations gradually disappeared and the sad outcome of this was that it gave employers even greater freedom to exploit juvenile labour.

The commencement of the eighteenth century saw the Act of Union between England and Scotland; henceforth the history of the two countries was to be more strongly entwined than ever before. By common acceptance it was now that the British trade union movement was born; its ancestry has been traced by some commentators from the journeymen guilds of the sixteenth and seventeenth centuries. And bearing that history in mind, it is hardly surprising that a movement with such a heritage should at times, even to this day, look upon the industrial world with a restrictionist eye. And if there is in fact a long-term 'folk-memory' within the trade union movement of our day, then the employers' and legislators' actions in the crucial years of the eighteenth and nineteenth centuries were not of a

---

[18] Sir J. H. Clapham, *A Concise Economic History of Britain from Earliest Times to 1750* (Cambridge University Press, 1943), p. 187.

nature to help in producing an outward-looking movement – past experience has taught that when the boot is on the other foot, little mercy may be expected.

The State's powers were used against working men who organised so as to protect their position. Examples are numerous; thus in 1719 workmen were forbidden from taking their skills abroad. And in 1726 there followed an Act which repressed the combination of workers; this included powers to transport workers for up to fourteen years for using violence in labour disputes and death for wilful machine-breaking. Yet, according to Adam Smith,[19] employers could combine 'with the utmost silence and secrecy to sink the wages of labour'. The situation was this: employers could prosecute individual workers for stopping work and bring action for conspiracy against members of trade unions.

Yet, despite all, special categories of workers, as, for example, engineers when the demand for machinery soared, earned boom wages at times.[20] Some quite strong trade unions existed amongst the skilled and the semiskilled, although these were quite often disguised as clubs or friendly societies, providing sickness and funeral benefits. With the increased mechanisation in the mid-eighteenth century it was possible to see higher wages and lower prices at the same time; consequently attitudes changed, the stress now being on improvement in the quality of labour that high wages could bring.[21]

THE LAST CENTURY

At the end of the eighteenth century, excesses across the Channel produced a reaction in this country, leading in turn to Pitt's Combination Acts of 1799 and 1800. There was a guise of respectability about the Acts, for they were supposed to cover masters as well as men; yet masters could in reality still combine as they wished, whilst the men were prosecuted for doing so. There were many instances of savage prosecution of workers under the Acts, yet it was not the law alone which prevented the majority of the unskilled labour force from entering into effective bargaining organisations: 'labour reserves were large enough to permit most employers to dismiss their discontented employees out of hand and to engage new men on the spot'[22] so that even after the Combination Acts were repealed, the workers were still without effective bargaining power – the result of this is not missed by today's well-read trade unionist. That which appears irrational to many an observer, such as resistance to "skills dilution", has its own rationality for the time-served craftsman and for his trade union representative.

And the state had not yet finished with the working man; in 1813 the

[19] A. Smith, *The Wealth of Nations* (Penguin, 1970), p. 93.
[20] P. Deane, *The First Industrial Revolution* (Cambridge University Press, 1965), p. 139.
[21] R. Mathias, *The First Industrial Nation* (Methuen, 1969), p. 201.
[22] P. Deane, op. cit., p. 149.

Elizabethan Statutes which gave the magistrates the power to enforce minimum wages were repealed. 'To leave the workman unprotected by the State as to wages, hours and factory conditions while denying him the right to protect himself by combination was frankly unjust.' [23] By the early eighteenth century, for practical purposes, the elaborate provisions of the Statute of Artificers affecting the regulation of wages and the training of skilled labour were completely ignored; when, in 1814, the Statute of Artificers was repealed, this was only regularising the existing situation. Now, to quote Lady Williams,[24] 'in many trades no questions were asked as to how long a journeyman had served, and masters took on as many young people as they wished without any form of either written or verbal agreement with regard to their training'. Professor Williams estimates that 99 per cent of journeymen working at the beginning of the nineteenth century would have been doing so illegally if the Statute had been enforced, yet the term 'apprentice' remained. The Poor Law authorities who in the early years of the last century farmed pauper children out to mills still spoke of them as apprentices. For pauper children the opportunity to obtain a real skill was not merely resisted by the owners but such craft organisations as there were also resisted such a course of events. Thus 'most trade societies in the mills tried to maintain the rule that only the children of relatives of the adult spinners could be trained in the mills as skilled spinners'.[25] The use of apprenticeship as a means of control is here clearly perceptible.

The anti-Jacobite period (1792–1822) had provided the Combination Acts; gradually it receded. Whilst Francis Place and Joseph Hume petitioned Parliament, the enlightened Peel was at the Home Office; in the years of 1824 and 1825 the Combination Acts were repealed and with it trade unionism was legalised and has never again been outlawed.

Even in the darkest days of the Combination Acts the skilled worker had many advantages over his less fortunate unskilled brother. Nor did the growth in population, the immigration from Ireland and the economic fluctuations on top of hostile laws permit the unskilled much thought of organisation. The skilled societies, which despite all had survived, had behaved in the eyes of authority in a responsible manner: 'their rules forbade violence and hostility to masters just as much as they sought to enforce a closed shop and prevent blacklegging between plants when there was a turnout'.[26] So the repeal of the Acts on the one hand formalised the existence of the craft clubs which in spite of the Acts had survived and on the other hand permitted organisations to the unskilled worker who had no experience of such bodies.

Trade unions now grew in numbers. There was much 'Utopian systems building'; and though much never got past the paper stage, Robert Owen's

[23] G. M. Trevelyan, op. cit., p. 483.
[24] G. Williams, op. cit., p. 1.
[25] R. Mathias, op. cit., p. 203.
[26] *ibid.*, p. 365.

'Grand National Consolidated Trades Union' of 1834 did achieve a membership of half a million before the ancient crime of 'oath-swearing' was invoked by those in authority in order to destroy it. Had Owen's idea of a nationwide multiskill general union succeeded, the 'force of tradition' which is one factor that still weds us to the apprenticeship system may possibly have been different, but this lies in the realm of speculation. As it was, 'during the nineteenth century the Trade Unions brought constant defensive pressure on the employers to limit the number of lads to each journeyman and to set a fairly advanced age (21 years) for the completion of training'.[27]

From the 1830s onwards there had been a temperance movement in Great Britain and alcohol was the great enemy of the working class. The cry was 'knowledge instead of alcohol'.[28] The 'new model unionism' of the 'amalgamated' unions was to be confined to sober, skilled workmen. The movement was evolutionary rather than revolutionary, its aim being to raise wages by barring all 'unapprenticed and insufficiently skilled' men. It is possibly paradoxical that more than 120 years later the same strategy is still used – even though the rate of technological change makes nonsense of the once-for-all approach to training for a skill.

The first of the new model unions was the Amalgamated Society of Engineers, founded in 1851, the year of the Great Exhibition, and barely three years after much of Europe had been torn by working-class revolution. Yet the restrictionist, harmonious, evolutionary concepts of these new bodies were very advantageous to its members. The five unions representing engineers, carpenters and joiners, iron founders, bricklayers, and boot and shoe operatives led the movement. The leaders of these unions, dubbed the 'London Junta' by the Webbs, were a truly powerful body. There are many indications of this power, and the official birth of the Trades Union Congress is dated from their attendance at the Manchester meeting of 1868, even though there had been conferences for some years previously, and it was the Junta which led the campaign for further legal recognition and for protection of trade unions – which were granted in statutes of 1871 and 1875. Here was a body which, unless driven to extremes, was always to be found on the conservative side of the trade union movement. Cole and Postgate [29] suggest that the amalgamated unions had three basic principles by which they abided and through which they operated: (a) wage war on intruders into the craft; (b) always come to an agreement with employers and deny any class struggle in action and in theory; (c) keep up high contributions for friendly society benefits. And the early 1870s were a period of boom, which accelerated the growth of skilled unions, especially in the larger industrial units – in the engineering shops and shipyards, the ironworks and railways, and in the mines. Money wages moved ahead of prices – vindication of the Junta's philosophy of industrial life.

[27] *Vocational Education* (OECD, 1967), p. 15.
[28] G. D. H. Cole and R. Postgate, *The Common People* (Methuen, 1938), p. 30.
[29] *ibid.*, p. 89.

With the 1889 London dock strike the unionisation of the unskilled 90 per cent of the labour force began in earnest. Certainly the process of unionisation of the British employed is hardly half-completed to this day. But the real growth since the last decade of the last century, ignoring the unionisation of the 'salariat', has been amongst the semi-skilled and un-skilled. To talk of the British union members as a homogeneous group is a mistake which the social scientist does not make. There are status groups akin to classes within the working class which have at times almost reached the stage of castes: not so very long ago to become a plater in a Clydeside shipyard frequently required a high degree of paternal nepotism – elitism through birth is not confined to the upper sectors of society.

When one considers the low wages of unskilled adult workers during most of the last century, it is easy to see why so few youths offered them-selves for apprenticeship. Poverty-stricken parents had little choice but to make their young sons into wage-earners as soon as possible. Apprentice-ship meant a financial sacrifice which many a parent was unable to under-take; if it was undertaken, then this was generally for one fortunate child from within the generally large families. And the industrial climate was hardly favourable: there was an increasing use of machinery for manu-facture and with it the demand for semi-skilled labour grew.

THE CHANGING SCENE OF MODERN CRAFTSMANSHIP

The history of the British trade union movement in the twentieth century as it affects manual workers has been one of growth and retrenchment, of general strike and of slump, of war and economic boom, and of post-war growth in membership numbers running concurrent with rationalisation, amalgamation and decline in the number of trade unions. Some unions, as for example the EETU/PTU (Electrical, Electronics and Telecommunica-tions Union/Plumbers Trade Union), have lost much of their craft bias. Others, such as the AUEW (Amalgamated Union of Engineering Workers), whilst their activity in the unionisation of those with lower skills has grown, have still kept a special place in the union hierarchy for those with appren-tice skills. Finally there are still unions, as for example the Amalgamated Society of Boilermakers, Shipwrights and Structural Workers, who cling to a great extent to the tight craft ideal of the earlier amalgamated societies, hardly surprisingly so, given the decline in shipbuilding in the United Kingdom, which makes a defensive stance almost inevitable.

The whole concept of craft unionism is changing. Single-craft unions are declining in numbers whilst multi-craft, industrial and general unions are increasing. There are many reasons for this, not least of all the rational-isation which is taking place within the British trade union movement at an ever-increasing pace. As we have seen, craft unionism was the first stable form of modern trade unionism to emerge. The advantages to members were due to the bargaining strength of the unions and their friendly benefits and were reinforced by the loyalties and traditions which these organisations engendered. And when 'at the end of the last century new theories of trade union organisation began to gain acceptance, these unions naturally showed no inclination to allow themselves to be carved up in response to theoretical argument'.[30] Yet, as we have seen, the movement has been towards multi-craft unions (some of which do admit less skilled workers of the trade), towards industrial unionisation and towards general unions.

We see today a situation where the majority of our industrial workforce do not possess any high-level manual skill, yet mechanisation, which has brought this state of affairs about, has also produced a demand for personnel with a very high degree of skill in order to make and maintain the very complex machines. For the latter a long period of apprenticeship often coupled with some measure of technical education was, until quite recently, a standard requirement. Yet systematic instruction was often lacking, nor were terminal tests applied in order to assess the quality of the training obtained; craft unions, as prisoners of tradition and in response to the need to defend their membership, were more concerned with length of training than with its quality, and employers by-and-large accepted the craft unions' definition of skills. The heirs of the craft unions have in the main not attempted to change the old traditions although the impact of the industrial training boards on this cannot be ignored, and trade unions can rightly claim to play their part here.

The power of industrial training boards, which were at one time perceived to be a possible major agent of change in the field of apprentice training, were curtailed in 1973 when a relatively low maximum levy on training was set and the intention was announced to phase out both training grants and levies. Yet much has already been achieved by some boards in both rationalising and shortening the apprenticeship period. The best example is to be found in engineering where the pertinent training board has produced a system of training 'modules'. This consists of first-year training in which all trainees take a broadly-based course concluding with a deeper application of the basic skills. At the end of this period a selection is made of one or more stage II modules of training, taking into account the needs of the firm and the capabilities of the individuals. This stage takes two to three months and may for example consist of basic welding or basic electrical practice. This is followed by suitable stages III and IV modules, which are modules of training for specialist skills. Typical stage III modules are metal-arc welding or electrical fitting; they take about six months to complete and there is no restriction on the number of stage III modules which may be taken. They are followed by a period of practical experience. In the view of the Engineering Industrial Training Board 'many craft trainees will be able to reach satisfactory standards of skill by the end of the third year of training, others might continue with further modules of training, and it should be understood that additional modules

---

[30] A. Flanders, *Trade Unions and the Force of Tradition* (University of Southampton, 1969), p. 29.

could be undertaken by any craftsman at later stages in their career'.[31] Stage IV modules are by and large an extension of stage III modules and again take about six months to complete. The minimum arrangement for any craftsman is one basic stage II module and any two of the stage III or stage IV modules. The board, which had previously levied at $2\frac{1}{2}$ per cent of pay roll and excluded from this only the smallest firms was, in 1974–5, excluding all engineering firms with emoluments of £150,000 or less and charging a 1 per cent levy on the year ending 5 April 1975. Obviously its powers, compared with previous years, had been seriously curtailed. As an aside it is interesting to note that the board does not refer to apprentices at all, but to 'craft trainees'.

Even though training boards are made up of employers, trade unionists and educationalists, the trade unions insist on minimum training periods. Thus in engineering in 1974 most apprenticeships took four years to complete, and only under very restrictive conditions was it possible to complete the training in three years. Paradoxically, some employers still insisted on a five years' apprenticeship; so trade union pressure is not wholly responsible for the lengthy training periods of apprenticeships.

In the construction industry the apprenticeship period at the beginning of 1974 was four years, although discussions were then in progress to reduce this to three years, and this was the case for a variety of other industries. Technical education has become an important factor in the training of apprentices and the movement towards such vocational education has been especially marked in the period since the Second World War. Technical education has not, however, been an absolute requirement for apprenticeship, and many employers have paid little more than lip-service to it. Yet possibly the most astonishing growth was in the National Certificate courses. Until the Second World War most apprentices who availed themselves of technical education attended evening classes at the local technical college for a City and Guilds of London Institution course. Relatively few employers took any notice of certificates so obtained, and this despite the fact that 'apprenticeship is completed without proof of proficiency by mere lapse of time – technical courses are completed by examination'.[32]

After the war so-called 'day release' – generally one day per week at the technical college, paid for by the employer, supplemented by one evening per week – became more common. At the same time City and Guilds courses, which had been designed for the elite of craftsmen,[33] often took second place to National Certificate courses. Until relatively recently National Certificate courses, via Ordinary and Higher National Certificates with suitable endorsements, led to corporate membership of certain professional institutions, yet these courses were beyond the ability of most boys who attended technical colleges and colleges of further education.

[31] *Information Paper No. 11* (EITB, May 1967), p. 5.
[32] K. Liepmann, op. cit., p. 109.
[33] G. Unwin, *The Guilds and Companies of London* (Cass, 1963).

The courses themselves contained a high mathematical and theoretical content, not unlike that of a university pass degree.

More recently the National Certificate route to professional status has been largely closed; thus, for example, the chartered engineering institutions now insist on a university degree or a very high level examination set by the Council of Engineering Institutions for membership. The new Ordinary and Higher National Certificates are more descriptive and less mathematical in content and are meant for higher technician education. For the vocational education of craftsmen the examinations of the City and Guilds of London Institution, suitably modernised, have once more come into their own. The situation is therefore now much more rational than it was a few years ago.

The industrial training boards have, since their formation in the second half of the sixties, made the undertaking of vocational training, but not necessarily the passing of examinations, a necessary part of craft training. Yet there are still employers, especially smaller employers, who can ill afford to lose the services of an apprentice for one day each week during term time, and who prefer to forgo the training board grant, which is often dependent on permitting suitable 'day' release or some equivalent vocational education. Many of the apprentices so affected do appear to side with the employers on this issue; they are glad to have school behind them and do not relish returning to an educational establishment, if only for one day per week.

The history of craft apprenticeship, although long, has shown little uniformity. On logical grounds many craftsmen today, no less than in the past, could not claim a monopoly of skills. Other men who had not served an apprenticeship could by diligent application obtain equal if not higher skills. Yet the tradition of apprenticeship lingers and 'craftsmen', i.e. time-served men, are still, not only by trade unions but also by the public generally, held to possess skills of an order to which the non-apprenticed person can only aspire.

Chapter 3

Background to Adult Training

The pace of technological change must inevitably sooner or later prove to the industrial labour force and the public at large that apprenticeship training may not provide a man with a skill which he will be able to use throughout his life. This situation is already clearly perceived by a variety of 'redundant' craftsmen whose skills are no longer required, as for example in the textile industry. A similar situation exists, although it is less obvious, when one considers the job being done, say, by some electrical fitters today; their training, received perhaps more than twenty years ago, may have made little mention of electronics, but now they use knowledge and skills mainly acquired on the job. The first of these two groups of craftsmen were forced to acknowledge that they required retraining; the second were fortunate enough to acquire their retraining whilst they worked. In the same way, there is a demand today for skills which were not envisaged twenty, or even ten, years ago. Examples of this are to be found among some instrument maintenance fitters and electronic test technicians. Realisation of this rapidly changing technological scene has been shown by the Engineering Industries Training Board's module system [1] which would allow an engineer to add a new 'block' to his qualifications should the marketability of his present skill become in doubt. However, the full use of the module system is still in the realms of the future and there is no guarantee that in practice the system will succeed. Apart from this scheme, we found little evidence that apprenticeship training programmes have made full provision for possible redundancies in the trade in the future.

This failure of the apprenticeship system to show adaptability results in the need for an institution capable of retraining adults who are redundant and to train men for the skills which industry requires of them. This is a role which government training centres [2] could fill, although there are many stumbling blocks in the way of their success in doing so.

One of these stumbling blocks is the rather chequered career which

[1] For a discussion of this scheme see Chapter 2.

[2] These centres have been called 'skill centres' since April 1974 but are referred to throughout by the name used during the research period.

40

government training has had since its inception in 1917 when 'instructional factories' were set up to train disabled ex-servicemen. In 1925 these centres were adapted to cope with the large numbers of unemployed. It was at this time that the centres fell into some disrepute for, in the depressed labour market, it was often not possible for the trainees to get jobs and so training was frequently seen merely as a device to keep men occupied for several months rather than as an opportunity to train for a new career. Prior to the outbreak of the Second World War the centres came into their own by training large numbers of urgently needed munitions workers. These trainees were employed under 'relaxation agreements' between employers and trade unions. These agreements allowed that when no time-served craftsmen were available, 'dilutee' labour might be employed but with the provision that such persons were allowed to tackle only specific jobs and to use only specific machines; details of such employees were to be noted in a 'dilution book'. At the end of the war the centres were occupying partly a social role in rehabilitating disabled ex-servicemen, but also an economic role in training men who had missed the opportunity to learn a skill. Training at that time was mainly geared to filling vacancies for skilled men in the construction industry. This work continued until 1947 when economic cutbacks, combined with a severe winter, threw many construction workers out of work. Unions, understandably, complained of the training of 'dilutees' when craftsmen had no work and so the number of government training centres was reduced and training restricted to ex-servicemen, unemployed and disabled men. This situation persisted until 1963 when, in response to persistent shortages of skilled labour, the Government began a continuous programme of expansion resulting in a total of 52 centres offering about 11,000 training places in 1972.

The types of training course offered by the centres reflect their history. Some courses are suitable for disabled people, e.g. watch and clock repair, hairdressing, and typewriter repair. Some courses are for the purpose of training men for skills required by industry and which are not yet covered by apprenticeship schemes, e.g. electronic wiring and instrument maintenance. The majority of courses, however, offer training for jobs normally filled by those who have served an apprenticeship, e.g. in the construction and engineering trades. These courses aim to provide in six to twelve months the basic knowledge required for a trade. Once the basic principles are learnt by the trainee he still requires on-the-job experience to enable him to complete his training. In some trades, as for instance agricultural fitting, joinery and bricklaying, arrangements are made for the trainee to be employed as an 'improver' over a period of sixty weeks. During this period he is paid an increasing percentage of the skilled wage rate, and the employer receives a small grant from the Department of Employment for his part in the training. In other trades, including engineering, the trainees, upon leaving the training centres, are left to gain experience on their own and may have some difficulty in building up acceptable production speeds.

These government training centre courses are no longer confined to the disabled and those with employment difficulties, but are now frequently (especially in times of low unemployment) used by men who come from regular jobs. Acceptance to most of the training courses is based on an interview by a selection 'panel'. Some of the more technically orientated courses, e.g. radio and television repair, also have a written educational test, but no use is made of any aptitude or vocational guidance tests. Admission to the course is as soon as possible thereafter, but the waiting list for some courses may be very long. If a man is prepared to live away from home during training it may be possible for him to cut the waiting period. In some cases men have to attend training centres away from home and free accommodation is then provided for them. Entry to most courses is 'staggered' with one or two men joining the course for a given skill each week; in addition to enabling full use to be made of the equipment available at the centre, this allows the instruction to be given on an individual basis. Another advantage here is that there is not a 'flood' of trainees from one trade and centre entering a local labour market at any one point in time. This aids placement, which would be more difficult if a large number of men were all seeking employment in the same skill and area. Some of the more technical courses have 'block' entry as these classes require much more theoretical instruction than the other mainly practical classes. The release of a class of this grade of worker did not appear to affect adversely the employment prospects of our trainees, but they may have been fortunate in that they had been trained for jobs which were in high demand such as in radio and television repair.

During their period at a government training centre the men are paid a tax-free training allowance. The allowances have always been slightly higher than the unemployment benefits which these men could expect to collect, but recent adjustments have made them considerably higher than unemployment benefit and therefore, in theory at least, very attractive. Men who have to live away from home have accommodation provided for them and those who travel each day have their expenses refunded. At the end of the training period men in certain trades are provided with a set of tools.

Plans are now under way to increase the level of training activity still further and the aim is to train over 60,000 men and women in 1975 and a figure of 100,000 is envisaged by the end of the decade. Previously the centres have been small producers of skilled labour; the 1972 figure represents only a fraction of the number of apprentices who finished training that year. It is difficult to foresee accurately what the future role of the training centres will be; at present they hope to rectify imbalances in the supply of skilled labour. Whether they will be seen as rivalling the apprenticeship system when their activity increases, only the future will show.

The value of these accelerated courses of training can be easily appreciated. Despite the organisation required to set up new courses it is still possible to institute a course and train men well inside the four years or so that would be required at present to train more craftsmen via the apprenticeship system, and the quota system of apprenticeships might not even permit the training of the increased number of apprentices which may be required. Adult training has the additional advantage of not restricting its recruitment to boys under the age of seventeen years or so, but rather of being open to anyone with the requisite ability. As a result, it should be possible to speedily supply the skilled men which industry needs, which should relieve the situation where increased production can be hampered by 'shortage of skilled manpower', a reason often quoted in the Confederation of British Industry's 'Industrial Trends Survey'. Naturally the trade unions, which know from bitter experience that skills shortages in times of high economic activity can become a surfeit in times of slumps, may view the situation differently. In times of high economic activity when there may be these shortages of skilled manpower the government training centres can play the role discussed above, but when the economy is depressed they have in the past tended to revert to the more social role of occupying the unemployed. It must be remembered that the men trained in government training centres are often 'marginal' employees who are hired only when no time-served men are available because, as well as possible prejudice from the existing work-force, the employer must face the initial problem of building upon the man's basic knowledge to bring him up to the experienced workers' standards of quantity and quality of output. This means that the trainee is in a difficult position in the labour market when unemployment levels are high. The training is then a social benefit, occupying the man for six or twelve months during a time when he might have been continuously unemployed and the theory is that when industrial activity picks up again the man should be able to use his new training. Whether or not this is the case will be demonstrated later in this book, when the effects of unemployment on a man released from training will be discussed. The ideal situation would be to commence training men six months ahead of an upsurge in employment, but this would require manpower forecasting at a level of sophistication which is not yet possible.

The marginality of a trainee's position in the labour market reflects back to the war-time situation of 'dilutees'. In these cases the rules were that the dilutee would be employed only if there were no time-served men available. Should time-served men become unemployed it would then be necessary to discharge the dilutee and to hire the time-served man instead; in this way trade unions tried to show generosity at the time when the nation faced a major emergency without forgoing their function of control in order to safeguard the livelihood and standard of living of their existing members. This situation still exists in theory under the rule books of the AUEW (Amalgamated Union of Engineering Workers), so that the situation could arise where a dilutee, trained over twenty years ago, would have to forfeit his job for a twenty-year-old craftsman. Although other trade unions now make no ruling on dilution, the inherited traditions may persist. The industrial areas in which a trainee has more guarantee of secure employment will be those with no such traditions, when he does not compete with large numbers of time-served men, as for example in radio and television repair.

This insecurity of employment of a trainee is a real danger which should not be minimised. The prospective government training centre recruit who is in employment ought to be given the facts so as to allow him to make an informed decision on whether to remain in what may be a dead-end job or to give up secure employment and gamble on the hope that he may, after training, gain access to a field of employment offering greater potential.

Most other industrialised countries have schemes for training adults which vary according to the labour reserves of these countries, to the traditions of craft training and to the existence and strength of pertinent trade unions. The country which is most often held up as an example here is Sweden, whose system has often been praised for its flexibility and success. The scheme does not differ significantly from that in the UK, but the environment in which it is set does. Permanent training centres are set up in areas of high unemployment and also in areas of high population density which may not necessarily have employment problems. As the aim of the system is flexibility, many courses are also offered in temporary training centres located in areas which may have short-term employment difficulties. Trainees may, however, have to move to centres away from their home areas if the course they want is not available locally. One difference in the Swedish as compared to the British system in normal times is the high number of unemployed who apply for training: in 1971 almost three-quarters of the male trainees (70.7 per cent) had been without work or in danger of losing their jobs. The success rate of the courses at this point in time was not remarkable; in the first three months of 1971 only 56.6 per cent of the 15,188 men and women trained were placed in related employment. Details of another 15.9 per cent are not known so these figures could be slightly higher, but the depressed employment situation in Sweden at that time makes this seem unlikely. This suggests that training 'success' even in a country with Sweden's record is dependent upon a buoyant economy. One interesting point is that there is no difficulty in gaining union acceptance for the trainees because of the lack of traditional apprenticeship training in Sweden. Craft training for youths is usually given in state vocational schools and few school-leavers embark upon an indentured apprenticeship.

Results available showing success rates of adult training in France relate to a period when skilled labour was in short supply. A survey of trainees four years after their training in 1960 showed that only 10.9 per cent of the group had made no use of their new skill and two-thirds were still in jobs which made use of their training. The French training scheme is another which has devoted its energies to training the unemployed; in that country youth unemployment is the problem – adult unemployment being not so common. Provision is also made to train members of the disadvantaged groups such as immigrants, handicapped or redundant workers. Various types of training courses are offered at the many centres throughout the country and assignment to a course can be via a 'clearing-house' system which may cut down the waiting time before training can begin, although this does depend on the trainee's willingness to live away from home. In addition to courses on two skill levels, one for skilled craft workers, the other for technicians, there are courses for young workers in order that they may experience various work situations before choosing their trades. The status of the French trainee at this time does not seem to be in much doubt because of the chronic shortages of skilled manpower in the country. If the demand for skilled men were to ease, it is not known whether the men trained in government centres would be at a disadvantage compared with men trained by industry.

In Germany the attitude towards adult skills training is ambivalent. There, training is undertaken on a similar basis to that in the UK, except that the end of training is marked by a trade test administered 'by the relevant guild'.[3] The German Federal Institute of Labour is not inclined to make any statement on the trainees' recognition by trade unions, although 'legally the trainee who has completed his training by passing the trade test set by the appropriate guild has equality with the skilled worker who has acquired his training through the normal apprenticeship'.

A similar situation exists in Canada where trainees also sit trade tests at the end of training, and for some workers recognition as qualified tradesmen is then given. However, 'gaining admission to the appropriate union is not easy for many graduates, particularly during periods of high unemployment when many union members are unemployed'.[4] The control function of trade unions, which is here used to safeguard the livelihood of existing members, can clearly be perceived.

Adult training is important in Canada as one quick way of making good the damage to the supply of skilled workers caused by the decrease in immigration of craftsmen into Canada. Also, because of its vast size, Canada is particularly vulnerable to short-run imbalances in the supply and demand for labour which, in a smaller country, might be solved by geographical mobility. Training is undertaken by provincial authorities in a wide variety of centres and is co-ordinated by the central government via the Canada Manpower Training Program. Entrants to the courses come from a wide variety of backgrounds, employed and unemployed. Those from employment may be learning a skill for the first time, but may also be using the training scheme as a means of obtaining a change of job or career. Training activity is highest in periods of seasonal unemployment, i.e. in the period January to March, and is low in April to August. Although selection is careful, placement appears to be poorly organised; many trainees drop

[3] Description of occupational training in the Federal Republic of Germany given by Der Bundesminister für Arbeit und Sozialordnung der Bundesrepublik Deutschland (1971).
 [4] Letter from Department of Manpower and Immigration, Ottawa (Oct. 1971).

out of courses as jobs become available while others return to their local manpower centres to register for unemployment.

Although variations occur in the organisation and details of the adult training schemes in different countries, all have one thing in common: the recognition that shortages of skilled manpower have a stunting effect on the growth of the economy. It is realised that accelerated vocational training offers a solution for the situation where large numbers of unemployed exist side by side with an unfilled demand for skilled workers.

Chapter 4

Investment in Human Capital:
The Meaning of Skill

INTRODUCTION

The history of apprenticeship illustrates the common acceptance that the skills of a 'time-served' man differ qualitatively from all other manual skills; yet without systematic instruction time-serving may have little in common with skills acquisition. So we are left with a categorisation of manual skills which depends on the existence and continuation of apprenticeships – and their acceptance by the relevant trade unions – even though the quality and quantity of training given can differ quite dramatically between one apprenticeship and another. Such a situation is likely to produce great anomalies, as for example that applying to welding skills in shipbuilding. In the construction and engineering industries electric-arc welding is normally accepted as being a semi-skilled job, requiring at most a six months' training period. In shipbuilding the trade is, however, viewed as one which requires a full apprenticeship. Some welders in shipbuilding may possibly require a much greater degree of skill than welders in other industries; but the opposite could equally well be true. Why then is this difference in emphasis placed upon the skill of welding? The reasons for this which are stated by many trade unionists are that in the non-ship-building industries the welding-torch is viewed as a tool, and single-tool skills are often accepted as of semi-skilled calibre, whilst in the shipyard welding is accepted as a trade. This then warrants a trade union struggle for wage differentials in favour of those welder members of the Boiler-makers' Society (the Amalgamated Society of Boilermakers, Shipwrights and Structural Workers) who are employed not only in shipyards, but also on construction sites, where members of other trade unions doing fairly similar jobs are thought to be semi-skilled. It may well be true that many shipyard-trained welders have skills of a higher calibre than welders trained elsewhere, but sometimes the opposite could be equally true. Thus the definition of 'skill' is even now [1] very much dependent on trade union acceptance, frequently on the basis of past history. Yet not past history alone, for given the decline of the British shipbuilding industry, it is hardly

---

[1] This is a period of rapid change; many of the future changes will be due to the activities and decisions of the various industrial training boards. This is discussed later.

surprising the guardians of its skilled labour force take up a defensive stance. When time-served men's jobs are perceived to be in jeopardy, the problem of control to safeguard the existing jobs is one which must inevitably exercise the minds of the trade union organisers, for it will surely be very much a felt problem of the rank and file membership. Here, in the words of C. Wright Mills, 'private troubles will become public issues'.[2]

Change is part of industrial life; inventions were made in all ages but the rate of change is without question faster now than ever before. With change in technology there must be changes in the skills requirements of industry. That skills are changing is in any event an observable fact; for example, modern machine tools for screw-thread rolling or gear-cutting do not require the intricate operating skills which the more rudimentary machines of twenty or more years ago needed. Or again, today's garage mechanic replaces faulty parts with factory-made or factory-reconditioned spares – which is a far cry from the skills possessed by the pre-war mechanic who had to be able to repair faulty parts, to 'blue and scrape' main and big-end bearings and so on, and the mechanic of yesteryear has to a large extent become a mere fitter in the true sense of that word. Again, few carpenters and joiners employed on building sites are now required to make window-frames or staircases, and doors are almost universally factory-made by semi-skilled labour. So skills requirements are changing, yet training times change only slowly and often only after considerable effort on the part of the industrial training boards. Yet Professor Williams stated in 1963 [3] 'it is nonsense to assume that every skill takes exactly the same time to master'.

Many jobs, then, are being partially deskilled but are nonetheless accepted as requiring an apprenticeship, whilst other jobs which have only arisen in the last few years are not defined as skilled and do not demand a formal apprenticeship, even though the skills requirements of such jobs may be of a high order. For example, some of the work in the manufacture of electronic instruments, such as those used for testing, has no formal training scheme and training programmes are arranged by individual companies.

It is now seen that craftsmanship is defined mainly on the basis of apprenticeship and much more tenuously on the basis of ability to perform. Training is left to the apprentice's firm – the union 'does not concern itself with the adequacy of the training but accepts the endorsed indenture as sufficient for issuing the ex-apprentice the "skilled ticket" which entitles the worker to the wage rates of the craftsman'.[4] The 'skilled ticket' obtained at the end of the period of indentured service is an instrument which will, the apprentice hopes, give life-long job security.

Let us leave aside for the moment the standards set by the industrial training boards, for their requirements are not absolutely binding in that they cannot be enforced beyond the grant/levy which may in any case

[2] C. Wright Mills, *The Sociological Imagination* (Penguin, 1970).

[3] G. Williams, *Apprenticeship in Europe* (Chapman & Hall, 1963), p. 6.

[4] K. Liepmann, *Apprenticeship* (Routledge, 1960), p. 140.

cease to exist in due course.[5] The quality of different craftsmen who in the eyes of the public and of the trade unions are expected to be identical or at least very similar can in fact be very different indeed, for no uniform test is applied to all apprentices of a given trade; in fact often no test at all is applied either during or at the end of an apprenticeship. Yet in other countries tests are an integral part of skills training,[6, 7] and the suggestion that in this country, too, apprenticeships ought to require a trade test before the apprentice is accepted as a craftsman has been made on numerous occasions in the past.[8]

THE PRESENT SITUATION

The situation at the moment is as follows. The definition of what bundle of skills shall be accepted as worthy of an apprenticeship is the prerogative of trade unions which use apprenticeships for the purpose of categorisation [9] into trades and non-trades. The training, however, is left very much to the employers as are the number of trainees. Maximum numbers are the province of trade unions in so far as trade unions often put a limit on the apprentices/journeymen ratio as a technique of control. But as employers cannot be forced to take apprentices against their will, minimum numbers cannot be enforced by trade unions. Indeed it is very doubtful whether unions are much interested in minimum numbers of apprentices. They are much more concerned with preventing a glut which could lead to unemployment and a reduction of earnings, which is a perfectly understandable strategy for trade unions to follow, yet may lead to a chronic shortage of certain skills to the detriment of the economy.

Time is of the essence with apprenticeships: time in terms of a clearly specified age-range during which an apprenticeship may be undertaken, and time in terms of a period of servitude in order to obtain the 'skilled ticket'. The Donovan Commission [10] had this to say about the craft system:

'... precise and rigid boundaries between ... craft and semi-skilled grades of labour can be settled only on an arbitrary basis ... the knowledge that

---

[5] Industrial training boards were established under the authority of the Industrial Training Act of 1964 in order to supervise the whole range of training in each board's particular industry. At this time industrial training boards levy firms above a certain size on the basis of the firm's payroll or on a *per capita* basis and then pay back grants in relation to the actual training of the firm's personnel. This power to levy was severely curtailed in 1973 and is in due course to be phased out.

[6] *Vocational Training in the Soviet Union* (BACIE, 1963).

[7] G. Williams, op. cit.

[8] See for example A. Rodgers. 'Now Test Industrial Training', *New Society*, Vol. 7, No. 171 (1966).

[9] And for purposes of identification; thus R. Brown and R. Brannan, 'Social Relations amongst Shipbuilders', *Sociology*, Vol. 4, No. 2 (May 1970): 'apprentice training not only transmits the skills and mystery of craft but also leads to a clear social definition of group membership. . . .'

[10] *Royal Commission on Trade Unions and Employers Associations*, Cmnd 3623 (1968), pp. 87–8.

they have virtually committed themselves to a craft for life makes men alert
to guard what they consider to be their own preserve. . . . In the context of
technological change the drawbacks of the craft system become even more
marked. It is unreal to assume that the demand for any particular range of
skill will be constant. If the only normal method of entry into the craft is
via an apprenticeship, supply will respond slowly and inadequately to the
demand. Thus the definition of skill as based on the craft system is found
inadequate and arbitrary, the defensive stance against change is seen as
virtually guaranteed because of it, and supply and demand are likely to be
in inequilibrium because of the existence of the apprenticeship system.'

Apprentices have always in the past been underpaid and even today they
are relatively badly paid; a situation which produces attitudes which are
likely to last a lifetime. Not infrequently the real training is completed
within the first few months of the commencement of an apprenticeship;
thereafter the boy may be put on 'skilled' work but at a low wage, thereby
being exploited and being aware of this exploitation. Yet, paradoxically,
other trainees are put on payment-by-results schemes, which may teach the
apprentice that no matter what the text-books or his day-release course
teachers may say to the contrary, the quality of work to aim for is the
minimum one can get away with.

The very term 'apprentice' may inhibit retraining and technological
innovation. There is a degree of inevitability about this when an apprenticeship means a lengthy period of servitude at low wages – this is then seen as
an investment, the returns of which are a (hoped for) lifetime of job
security and favourable pay differentials, as well as high status in the social
stratum of manual workers. This is of course not unique to apprenticeship
training; those who undergo training for a profession do so for similar
reasons. Nor, of course, is the situation unique to this country, as the
following indicates: [11] 'Four thousand years ago apprenticeship was recognised as the best way to train someone as a skilled craftsman. Today . . . it
is still so.' Another publication by the same American body [12] suggests that
the ratio of journeymen to apprentices should not, in the main, be less than
three to one. So in this context the situation in the USA is not very dissimilar
to that in the UK, and skill is again defined by indentured apprenticeship.

The whole philosophy behind apprenticeship leads inexorably to elitism,
which makes it almost axiomatic that only a minority of young men (albeit
a significant minority) – and far fewer young women, for whom apprenticeships are unusual – will obtain an apprenticeship. But for those who do
there is the hope of job security, favourable pay differentials and status.
The European tradition of apprenticeship is closely allied with craft
unionism and that tradition has even succeeded in crossing the Atlantic.

[11] From *Apprenticeship Training* (US Department of Labor/Manpower Administration leaflet, 1969).
[12] *Setting up an Apprenticeship Program* (US Department of Labor/Manpower
Administration leaflet, 1969).

The spiritual home, however, of craft unions, is to be found in this country. Thus 'craft unions, like the craft itself, may have been originally founded on the system of apprenticeship, but the interest of the union in this system was mainly directed to regulating entry into the trade, not to upholding certain standards of training. Control of the supply of competitive labour was the foundation of the early craft societies; without it no viable organisation could be sustained and none of the regulations could be enforced'. [13] Thus, once more, skills definition is based on apprenticeship rather than training, and control coupled to tradition is the matrix in which the roots of apprenticeship are to be found. Technical change is likely to bring stronger rather than weaker defence of the craft preserve, even though it may erode the genuine skills content of the craft. 'Indeed, the more notional the skills gap becomes, the greater the significance of the demarcation practices to the craftsman' for they 'are then more like the sea wall which stands between the inhabitants of the island and the total flood.' [14]

Few will now doubt that in defining skills in the traditional context of apprenticeships and craft unions we are facing a complex and emotionally loaded word. Perhaps, in order to aid understanding, it would be useful to commence with a series of definitions of skill, in the qualitative and quantitative sense, which does not rely upon tradition. Let us therefore put aside for the moment thoughts of apprenticeship and craft unionism and speak instead of training.

Firstly, there is the time element in training. The object of any training should be to impart the skills and knowledge of the job so that the job can be performed – in terms of speed and of quality – to experienced worker standard.[15] With the advent of systematic analytical training of 'operators' this has become accepted as the aim of any training course for male and female semi-skilled workers. The aim of experienced worker standard is no less pertinent to the higher skills, even though the diagnostics skills of many 'craftsmen' are of a more sophisticated order than the merely manipulative skills of the majority of operators.[16] Manual skills then consist of job knowledge in addition to manipulative skills, and the more sophisticated the skill the greater the diagnostic element is likely to be.

THE TRANFERABILITY OF SKILLS

A further subdivision, allied to the foregoing, is that of general versus specific skills.[17] This division is most useful when the problem of appor-

---

[13] A. Flanders, *Trade Unions and the Force of Tradition* (University of Southampton, 1969), p. 11.

[14] *ibid.*

[15] Experienced Workers Standards of speed and quality of work are the yardstick used by modern trainers to decide when training is complete. The terms are self-explanatory.

[16] See for example, W. D. Seymour, *Industrial Skills* (Pitman, 1966).

[17] G. Becker, 'Investment in Human Capital: A Theoretical Analysis', *Journal of Political Economy* (supplement, 1962), pp. 9–49. This subdivision has become standard terminology in the training field.

tioning training costs arises. General training may be defined as training which produces skills that have at least a sizeable transfer element, i.e. they are of use in many firms, irrespective of whether they have been obtained in a firm or in a vocational institution. In practice, completely general training will seldom be given by a firm – there would usually be a specific element in such training. If training is really general then it would be patently unfair to expect a particular firm to pay for all such training of a person; and one of the objectives of the Industrial Training Act when first introduced was precisely to spread such cost so that all the firms in an industry which could benefit would either do their fair share of general skills training or help by contributing to the cost of other firms which did more than their fair share of such training. As Becker maintains that under perfect competition the fully trained person has to be paid the full value of his marginal product – otherwise he would move on to another firm which would do so – one may ask how the firm can finance the training. The answer appears to be that the firm is able to pay the trainee less than the value of his marginal product during the training period, the difference financing the training. In effect the trainee pays for his own training, in the hope and expectation of obtaining a return on his investment later. In the British context some at least of the cost is borne by agencies other than the individual receiving the training – for example by the State or local authority when training takes place in government training centres or technical colleges. Craft apprenticeship training, if properly given, should contain a major general element. The same is true for training obtained in a government training centre.

Completely specific training 'describes the training which raises the trainee's productivity only in the training firm'.[18] Hardly any training is completely lost if a person moves from one firm to another; attitudes, manual dexterity, stamina, all these contain a transfer element. Yet some training is so tightly orientated towards the needs of a given firm that the largest proportion cannot be transferred. Johnson [19] sees the training of an operator to control a patented process as possibly coming nearest to completely specific training. Induction training is one form of specific training; other skills-training can be viewed as being more or less specific – each case should be judged on its own merits. Thus Becker: 'Clearly some kinds of training increase productivity by a different amount in firms providing the training than in other firms. . . . Completely specific training can be defined as [having] no effect on the productivity of trainees that would be useful in other firms. Much on-the-job training is neither completely specific nor completely general. . . .' [20] Thus training which is not completely specific may be viewed as comprising two elements: one being completely general and the other completely specific. And the proportion

[18] P. S. Johnson, 'The Economics of Training and the ITBs', *Moorgate and Wall Street* (Autumn 1971), p. 55.

[19] *ibid.*, p. 57.

[20] G. Becker, op. cit., p. 17.

of one to the other depends on the degree of skills transferability. In, for example, the case of surgical needle manufacture we are dealing with a skill which is so biased towards the specific training end of the general-specific continuum that the transfer element is minimal. In many well-conducted apprentice training schemes we are almost at the other extreme of the self-same continuum in that these are heavily biased towards general training.

It is not intended to describe non-manual skills; the above argument, however, applies also to this area of training. If we take, from the field of professional training, the case of the medical practitioner, it will be found that, even though much of the training is general, some specific training in, for example, learning the hospital routine or getting to know the patients, is necessary.

Who pays for specific training? It would appear that the firm has to pay for this, though it may sometimes be able to share this with the employee. And whilst theoretically the firm must pay the trainee a higher wage than he would be able to obtain elsewhere, this will in practice still be lower than the value of his product to the firm.

Becker's view is that a firm would behave rationally if it paid generally trained employees the same wage as they could obtain elsewhere, whilst specifically trained employees would get a higher wage-rate than is obtainable outside. In so far as a skill is really general, one skills-practitioner can easily replace another, whilst specific skills need to be taught from scratch when a new worker replaces one who has resigned. Firms should therefore be more concerned about labour turnover of employees with highly specific skills than with general skills. If this were so, then workers with specific skills ought to have greater security of tenure than those with general skills. Prima facie this is not so, yet a closer analysis may well indicate that those workers who possess a general skill of some significance which is in short supply, and who build upon this a specific skill – i.e. one which is heavily orientated towards a particular firm – have greatest job security. In dealing with job security it ought not to be overlooked that a view prevails which believes that transfer of training is an established fact; this *may* tend to make firms hold on to persons with sophisticated general skills in anticipation of easy retraining, should this become necessary.

A third point which needs to be considered is *where* the training should be given for maximum efficiency. Here a basic division which has common acceptance in the training field is between off-the-job and on-the-job training. General education, which is one aspect of investment in human capital, may be viewed as off-the-job training; the training given in apprentice training centres, in government training centres and in trade schools are all aspects of off-the-job training. On-the-job training is, as the term implies, given whilst the person – often under supervision – attempts to assimilate at the actual work station the intricacies of the tasks which are to be his job. In recent years the term 'sitting by Nellie' has been applied to on-the-job training.

Even when a significant or major part of the training has been given off-the-job, training on-the-job will have to be provided before training can be considered completed. Thus a growing part of apprenticeship training is given in training schools and the like; but no such training can be considered completed before the apprentice has been successfully fitted into the working situation. A similar argument holds for government training centre trainees, and one criticism voiced by the trainees with whom this book is concerned was that at this time too little is being done in order to acclimatise these 'adult apprentices' to the actual working conditions [21] which will face them on leaving the training centres. This mixture of off-the-job and on-the-job training is found in all sorts of training situations; it applies equally to the training of professional workers, as for example, lawyers and dentists, and also to managers and supervisors, as to the training of manual workers.

SKILLS DEFINED

The problem with defining skills is that definitions which on the face of it should be open to objective analysis are on closer inspection very much determined by those who hold power in society. Even a cursory analysis will indicate that the elitist concept of 'professionalism' is decided by those who can marshal a high measure of esteem and power. This problem is far beyond the scope of this book, yet some definitions are necessary if we are to make sense of the complex situation facing us and the following may be perceived as an attempt to bring some order into the subject as it affects the industrial situation covered by this book. The suggestions put forward so far are that the acquisition of manual skills may, for analytical purposes, be usefully viewed outside of the context of apprenticeships and craft unions – though this is not, of course, to suggest that there are no functions for either. Patently there are, otherwise they would have disappeared long ago. But skills can then be seen for what they really are and suitable training arrangements made in order to produce the requisite skills. The objective factors which can then be analysed are:

1. The mixture of diagnostic and manipulative skills (i.e. the appreciation of what is 'wrong' as well as the ability to put it 'right') – including job knowledge, i.e. the theoretical knowledge required in order to cope successfully with the individual job. Generally speaking, the more complex jobs have a higher diagnostic content, which in turn requires a more sophisticated training approach.

2. The mix of general and specific skills of a given job. These concepts allow us in theory at least to apportion training costs between trainee and

---

[21] This shortcoming in their training was almost universally experienced by the ex-trainees who made up the main sample of the research, as was clearly indicated by the many pertinent comments voiced by ex-trainees.

employer, and may also provide us with an additional yardstick for wage-rate decisions.

3. On-the-job and off-the-job training. Here the suggested decisive factor is not where such training has been done in the past – tradition can put our thinking here into a straitjacket – but rather where it ought to be done for maximum efficiency. Only experience will provide the knowledge which can be used for this. Most jobs benefit from a mixture of both types of training; it is not normally an either/or decision but rather one of obtaining the correct balance.

4. It is most important that there be an assessment of the efficiency of training and selection by means of tests. Training schedules should be so broken down that there is continuous assessment; then corrective action may be undertaken in order to improve the performance of the trainee – or of the training programme – well before the end of any training course.

All training is wasted if it is not directly related to the needs for specific skilled manpower. Industry will have to decide its skills requirements and therefore its training needs well in advance. There is a need for better manpower forecasting, manpower planning and manpower development. The fault here lies often outside the decision-making processes of the individual firm, which may see its well-laid plans destroyed by the stroke of a pen in Whitehall. The need for more intelligent planning is on the macro-level as well as on the micro-level; for the economy and for a given industry as well as for an individual firm. That this does not function well is easily observed; yet it should not be beyond the wit of man to devise plans which are realistic enough to have some hope of achievement. The post-war era is littered with national plans and national growth targets which were either badly thought out or had, for some other reason, to be soon abandoned.[22] National plans are the responsibility of the political system. Industry-wide manpower forecasting ought then to be attempted within this framework, and should be the function of the pertinent industrial training board which, given its composition of trade union as well as employer and educationalist members, could take due notice of the interests of the existing pool of labour with the requisite or retainable skills. For individual companies the planning of manpower requirements and the assessment of training needs cannot be separated; they are part and parcel of the same activity.

Individual firms should follow good management practice and set company objectives and should also define their strategies for reaching these objectives, always bearing in mind the interests of the existing labour

[22] This is not to suggest that long-range economic plans can ever hope, excepting by fortuitous accident, to achieve their aim with a high degree of accuracy. Indeed it will be argued that training facilities such as government training centres serve the useful function of making planning mistakes good. But it is a plea to attempt at plans which are produced not by politicians in moments of euphoria but rather with the use of the best planning techniques at hand.

force, otherwise understandable resistance from that quarter must be expected. This may then produce some congruence between the manpower plan and its achievement. This is not to deny that all plans are likely to suffer some degree of failure, for the future is not easily accurately foretold; the vagaries of the economic climate have their effect at all levels of the planning, and they often stem from international sources. Government intervention on doctrinaire as well as economic grounds should be mentioned as another cause for blowing plans off-course. And innovation, which can have the most dramatic effects on manpower requirements, is often difficult to anticipate. Obviously short-term plans, say of one to three years' duration, stand a much better chance of realisation than do longer-term plans; yet both kinds of exercise are well worth while conducting. It could be mentioned here in passing that, despite the voluminous amount of lip-service rendered to 'manpower planning', a recent survey undertaken by the Manpower Studies Research Unit which conducted the research described in this book indicated that relatively little real manpower planning is being undertaken by a major proportion of British industry. It is hardly surprising that a policy of 'hire and fire' leads to resistance by the working force. Given the structure of British industry, it may well be inevitable that some firms are from time to time forced into a hire and fire tactic, but this is hardly a good strategy for better industrial relations. Finally, the existence of training facilities to make good any faults in the manpower plans and its consequent imbalance in the supply of skills is imperative. This points to the importance of facilities such as government training centres and any resistance to the full integration of personnel trained in such establishments is almost bound to be dysfunctional to the economy.

At the turn of the century there was undoubtedly a clear-cut distinction between the skilled and unskilled workers in manufacturing industries. Since then, increased mechanisation and specialisation have led to the deskilling of many traditional crafts; with the changes in organisational structure of firms, many of the traditional craft skills which were required to make a product have, in the intervening period, moved from the shop floor into the offices which deal with the preparatory stages. Even now the terms 'technician' and 'technologist' are ill-defined; twenty-five years ago they were hardly used at all. It is the movement from the shop floor to office of the preparatory stages of production which has brought about much of this change. The training of technicians and technologists will not be discussed here in any detail, but some of the changes which the training of these grades is undergoing are mentioned. In the first two post-war decades the majority of technicians and technologists were trained outside the university sector of the educational system. For example, the part-time route – via Higher National Certificate and the like – was the most usual route to chartered engineering status. Now full-time education at universities and polytechnics has to a great extent supplanted this avenue to professional status so that the apprenticeship system now provides only a small proportion of the technologists and a diminishing (though still major) proportion of the technicians. Writing in the early 1960s Liepmann stated,[23] 'The apprenticeship system now embraces future technicians and technologists, even some scientists and various managerial specialists.' This view is now dated; with the increase in higher education many of the jobs now at the interface of the technician/technologist division which were previously filled by erstwhile apprentices are now sought after by graduates, and this movement is likely to accelerate as more and more graduates have to be placed in employment. The search for status by the various qualifying institutions, producing the movement towards 'graduate professions', is likely to prevent apprentices from moving up the ladder to the technologist rung. The increase in the number of young people obtaining full-time education may also mean that there are fewer of the academically able taking up youth apprenticeships. Allowing for the foregoing, one may have to rephrase the above quotation so as to make the cut-off point of an apprentice's career at below the technologist level excepting in very unusual circumstances. Line management is, however, still likely to recruit from among the apprentices (though not exclusively so), the normal route here being via first-line supervision.

We see then that skills categories change with time and so do recruitment sources for the various categories. It is suggested that the following categorisation may prove useful in defining industrial skills and its concomitant training requirements:

1. *Nominal absence of skills.* This would require little more than induction training, and possibly a very small element of on-the-job training. A production labourer is an example of this category.

2. *Simple one-job skills.* Here training requirements are to provide manipulative skills and very likely some limited job knowledge, as for example faults identification. Training may have a limited off-the-job element, but most of the training will be on-the-job. Many female operators' jobs would fall within this category.

3. *More complex one-job skills.* Manipulative skill is important and more complex than for (2) above, and generally the job-knowledge content of training is proportionately larger. Off-the-job training could occupy a significant though not major part of the training period. There may also be a small vocational education element. Production milling is an example here.

4. *Multi-job skills.* Training requirements will be for manipulative skills and for job knowledge, and can be seen as comprising a series of courses for (3) above. Additionally there may be a limited diagnostics content. Training will be a mixture of off-the-job and on-the-job, with an additional vocational education element. The ability to use a variety of production machines is an example, and this has often rated an apprenticeship in the past.

[23] K. Liepmann, op. cit., p. 20.

5. *'Craftsmanship' skills*. This is an extension of (4) above in that the diagnostics element has usually a much greater emphasis put upon it. Examples are tool-room fitter, jobbing plumber. Training will comprise on-the-job and off-the-job elements to give the requisite skills and experience; the vocational education element now becomes important.

6. *Technician*. Here the emphasis is on technical knowledge and, very likely, will contain a large diagnostics element, so training in the manipulative skills will be of less importance than for craftsmanship. Vocational education now assumes a very important role. Recruitment of technicians is likely to come from three sources:

(i) from (5) above – who are given further training and education;
(ii) directly from older school-leavers with the requisite qualifications and from other lower-grade (but *not* low-grade) workers who have enjoyed an extended secondary education;
(iii) from among those who have had a measure of higher education. Examples are draughtsmen and laboratory technicians.

7. *Technologists*. Here manipulative skills are hardly necessary; diagnostic skills are important, but not as important as for (6) above – technologists are supported by technicians. Job knowledge of a high order and especially a large measure of theoretical background knowledge become all-important now. Managerial skills which can be of some importance in (6) above, now assume a higher degree of significance, and the main source of recruitment is from personnel who have enjoyed a large measure of higher education, although some upgrading of technicians may be possible. Some off-the-job training may be given within the firm – for example as part of a postgraduate apprenticeship. Any on-the-job training is for job knowledge and to sharpen diagnostic skills. Example are systems analysts, research engineers, textile technologists.

Additionally there will be a need for office skills, professional skills, e.g. accountants, managerial skills, and so on, none of which is considered above. That list is meant to bring up to date the traditional division of our industrial labour force into unskilled, semi-skilled and skilled workers. Inevitably there is some overlap, for example the above list takes in some managerial and professional skills, but these are only coincidental. It will be noted that no age limits are suggested; only when it is found that there are age limits beyond which certain skills cannot be assimilated, should such limits be applied. Ignoring then the cost/benefit question of training people at different ages [24] it has to be accepted that young people do learn

---

[24] It is not intended to discuss the cost/benefit aspects of training and retraining – these are already well documented. See for example: J. J. Hughes, *Cost Benefit Aspects of Manpower Retraining* (DEP, HMSO, 1970); A. Ziderman, 'Cost Benefits of Adult Retraining in the United Kingdom', *Economica*, Vol. 36, No. 144 (1969), pp. 363–76; B. Thomas, J. Moxham, J. A. G. Jones, *A Cost Benefit Analysis of Industrial Training* (Report on an Enquiry for DEP, 1970).

more easily – if only because memory declines with age and 'memory plays an appreciable part in skills learning'.[25] But even then no rigid demarcation lines should be mandatory, for chronological age need not be a limiting factor on the learning process 'so long as you continue to learn – keep the machine oiled'.[26] And if our labour force does indeed enjoy regular doses of retraining, then the machine will be continuously relubricated.

Nor are training times suggested; the best training techniques are those which produce the requisite skills in the least time. The research effort now being put into learning theory as applied to the problems of skills acquisition is most likely to reduce training times by making training more efficient; the use of teaching machines, of simulated exercises and the like is bound to have an effect on training efficiency. And the use of trade tests cannot be over-emphasised; training without feedback is wasteful.

There is a real need for a well-educated labour force, for only on the foundation of a sound education can rapid, efficient training be built. This implies that the educational institutions are an important partner in a nation's training effort – i.e. it is they who start the process of investment in human capital. This is not to suggest that education is not more than this; obviously there is more to life than work, and it is the educationalists' job to help those under their charge to acquire those abilities and knowledge which are necessary in order to live a full life. But anyone who suggests that education in this country should not in any way be directed towards the needs of industry or its labour force is deceiving himself.

Skills acquisition, no matter of what level, is now seen as a cumulative process. The educational institutions play a crucial role; this means that every member of society should be educated to the limit of his or her ability. That part of education which has a vocational element may be viewed as an aspect of general training. Beyond the school – or university – some general training which extends a person's skills repertoire may be worthwhile, even if it is not immediately fully utilised; this may be viewed as a long-term investment. It must, however, be borne in mind that any skill which is not practised will suffer some degree of atrophy. Finally, on the sound foundation of a good education and some degree of general training is built the specific skills requirement of the job which is to be performed.

It has to be re-emphasised that training is not a once-for-all process. It never has been, but now with the accelerating pace of technological innovation it has to be accepted that the need for constant retraining – or further training in a skill which is evolving – is the order of the day. This indicates the importance of government training centres in which a major part of the country's retraining effort is likely to take place.

[25] E. Belbin, 'Adult Training and Retraining', *Industrial Training International* (August 1967).
[26] *ibid.*

PART II

THE DATA FROM THE LONGITUDINAL STUDY

Chapter 5

The Longitudinal Research Project
and its Methodology

The monitoring of adult training programmes in other countries occurs at different levels varying in sophistication and procedure. The USA has produced careful evaluations of its various programmes; included among them is the work of Gerald Somers and his collaborators.[1] France has also conducted follow-up studies of men who attended vocational training in order to evaluate the success of the training and the rate at which trainees leave their trades.[2] In this country, details of the numbers of trainees placed in jobs where they make use of their new skills are published regularly; yet these figures are not comprehensive and may omit men who obtained jobs by their own efforts after leaving government training centres. The real limitation of these figures, however, is that whilst they give information on what occurs immediately after training they do not answer many vital questions such as how long the first job is held, what wages the trainees earn, how earning power changes with on-the-job skills acquisition, and where the trainees work. In the mid-1960s an attempt to answer these problems was made by a government social survey, initiated by the Department of Employment.[3] Unfortunately, this survey was prone to the drawbacks which are liable to affect government enquiries no matter how well they may be designed; for example, despite guarantees of confidentiality an interview conducted by a civil servant or by somebody perceived to have connections with the civil service may produce not the true answer but the answer which the interviewee regards as the 'right' one.

In the autumn of 1967, discussions were begun with officials from the Scottish headquarters of the Department of Employment to consider initiating a study of the effects of government training on the supply of skilled labour in Scotland. The survey would follow the post-training employment success of trainees and would investigate firstly the effects

[1] G. Somers, *Retraining the Unemployed* (Wisconsin University Press, 1968).

[2] Jean, Gresez, *Enquiet pour Sondage sur la Réussite Professionnelle (1964) des Ancien Stragiaires F.P.A. sortis en 1960*, Ministère des Affaires Sociales, 1967.

[3] The department was known as the Ministry of Labour at that time and later as the Department of Employment and Productivity. It is referred to only by its present title, Department of Employment, for consistency.

which the acquisition of a skill in later life would have on a trainee and his family; secondly, the reasons which aid and those which prevent suitable men from coming forward for retraining, and thirdly, social mobility and geographical mobility of men after leaving government training centres. The proposed method of investigation was to interview men during their training at government training centres and to compare their progress – considering factors such as employment, earnings, geographical and social mobility – with the progress of other matched work groups over a period of approximately eighteen months. Pilot work and preliminary interviews were begun in the spring of 1968 and the granting of financial assistance from the Department of Employment allowed the project to proceed, utilising the previous work for piloting purposes throughout the remainder of the longitudinal research period – for example the final questionnaire was tried out on this initial group and, after modification, used on the main group of trainees.

Initially it was intended to study only trainees whose homes were in central parts of the east of Scotland, in the Lothians and Fife, so interviews were held at the two training centres in that area – Muircockhall in Dunfermline and Granton in Edinburgh. Later, to increase the number of trainees, visits had to be made to three other government training centres in Scotland: Hillington, Bellshill and Dumbarton, and a sample of men from all over Scotland, though still mainly from the east, was obtained.

Trainees were approached by a member of the government training centre staff and asked if they would help with the research project. Almost without exception, those approached in this way agreed to participate and arrangements were made for the trainees to leave their work for about one hour and to assemble in one of the lecture-rooms where a member of the research team met them. Once the purpose of the enquiry was explained, with great emphasis being placed on the confidential nature of the enquiry, co-operation was asked for and those not willing to participate were asked to withdraw at this point. The longitudinal nature of the survey demanded that all those interviewed should be prepared to keep in touch over an eighteen-month period with Heriot-Watt University where the research team was based. When agreement was given by the trainees, questionnaires were distributed together with a letter giving written confirmation of the nature of the survey and a guarantee of confidence. Each man filled in his own questionnaire while the interviewer explained what was required of each question and answered any problems as they arose.

Two hundred and eighty-seven trainees were interviewed in this way during their training courses. Of this number, twenty did not complete their courses, so were withdrawn from the sample. Later the death of one of the trainees reduced the numbers to 266, and it was this number which formed the survey sample.

The next contact with the trainees was made approximately six months after they completed training. The trainees finished their courses at intervals during the period July 1968 to July 1969, so each month contact was being made with those who had graduated six months previously. A very short questionnaire, requesting details of employment progress, was sent with a letter reminding the trainee of his commitment to the research, emphasising the importance of his participation and reinforcing the confidential nature of the enquiry. A prepaid envelope was enclosed for the reply. After one month, replies had been obtained from just over one-half of the group (54.5 per cent). A second letter similar to the first but suggesting that the trainee might have mislaid the questionnaire was sent out to the non-respondents. This contact brought the response rate to 74.1 per cent and a final reminder to the persistent non-respondents gave a response of 80.1 per cent to the first short questionnaire (see Table 5.1).

Approximately twelve months after the end of training this procedure was repeated with another short questionnaire. These first two postal questionnaires gave only brief details of the man's employment situation and although they were important in providing up-to-date information on the trainee's reception at work, their real purpose was to keep in touch so that when the final questionnaire was sent more than eighteen months after the first contact the trainee should not have forgotten about the enquiry. Another important use of these regular contacts was that any changes of address should be quickly realised and followed up so that, although some detective work was required anyway, the difficulties incurred were not those which might have been expected after a gap of eighteen months. To reinforce the idea that these questionnaires were merely friendly enquiries as to the trainee's progress, the second one was accompanied by a report of the results from the first eighty-seven questionnaires received from men who had left training centres six months previously. This report fulfilled promises by the research team to keep in touch with trainees and also encouraged those men who had not replied by showing that it was of interest to hear from all trainees whether they were using their training or not. This approach had the value of producing greater participation from the trainees, who volunteered much valuable information. Despite this, the response rate at the end of the twelve-month period dropped to 69.5 per cent.

TABLE 5.1   *Response rates of Scottish trainees to postal questionnaires*

Number interviewed initially: N = 266

	After initial letter	*After first reminder*	*After second reminder*	*After interview*
First postal questionnaire	145	197	214	n/a
	54.5	*74.1*	*80.1*	
Second postal questionnaire	117	166	185	n/a
	44.0	*62.4*	*69.5*	
Final postal questionnaire	119	155	187	258
	44.7	*58.3*	*70.3*	*97.0*

Note: Figures in italics are totals expressed as percentages of N.

The final postal contact with the trainees was made with a much longer questionnaire. As well as asking for details of employment the questions covered union membership, attitudes to government training, actual or intended geographical mobility and various indicators of social class. The non-repondents to this questionnaire were sent reminders in the usual way, but the second reminder suggested that it might be necessary or desirable for a member of the research team to visit the homes of those who did not reply. The response rate to this questionnaire at the end of the postal contacts was 70.3 per cent.

An attempt was made to contact all of the 79 trainees who had failed to reply to this final questionnaire. Senior university students were employed during their vacations to interview most of the men involved, as the trainees were scattered throughout Scotland, and it would have been beyond the financial resources of the project for the research team to attempt all the interviews. Before undertaking the work all student-interviewers attended a briefing meeting when it was made certain that they all understood the purposes of the research and the professional behaviour required by interviewers requesting confidential information. None of the students had previous experience of interviewing but this was not considered to be disadvantageous as their function was merely to supervise the completion of what had been designed as a postal questionnaire. Altogether 71 men were successfully interviewed, making a response rate of 258 men out of the total sample of 266 (97.0 per cent).

The mechanics of contact and follow-up were repeated for the five control groups in exactly the same way as for the trainee group. Description of the methods used in gathering these control groups is given below.

TRAINEE GROUP FROM LIVERPOOL

As the main group of trainees was made up of men from Scotland, which supposedly has a unique economic and cultural climate, it was thought that to interview a group of trainees from another development area would be useful. The resources of the project being limited, this was necessarily a small group which could only give a rough indicator of any differences between Scottish trainees and others. Thirty-seven trainees from Aintree Government Training Centre, Liverpool, formed this sample. Difficulties in maintaining the interest of this group were found because of the distance between Edinburgh and Liverpool, and because of the perceived Scottish bias of the research by the Liverpool trainees. This lack of involvement in the study by Liverpool trainees was demonstrated in their final response rate of 33 men, or 89.2 per cent of the group, a figure which in itself was only achieved after 29.7 per cent of the sample had been interviewed. Similar difficulties of raising interest in Reading to a mainly Scottish-based project have been met in another survey [4] where response rates

[4] Tom Burns, *Styles of Life and Occupational Mobility* (Final Report to SSRC, March, 1970).

were low due to resistance to a project which 'was not of tangible value to the Reading community'. It would seem necessary for the ideal inter-regional comparison to have centres in both areas under study. Information from the Liverpool group did not show any significant differences between it and the Scottish group so that, in the absence of any other evidence, it is assumed that the findings of the Scottish survey are mainly true for other development areas in the UK and in a large measure for the whole of the country.

Four categories of manual workers were chosen to act as control groups for trainees in measuring any changes in social and geographical mobility and to give comparative information on earnings levels over the study period. The four categories of men chosen were time-served craftsmen, final-year apprentices, operators and unemployed men.

Craftsmen

The hypothesis forwarded at the beginning of the study was that craftsmen would represent the ideal towards which the trainees would aim. After their training at government training centres, the trainees would be looking for jobs normally held by time-served men and would be competing in the skilled labour market. It was intended that the craftsmen would act as indicators of how close the trainees came to equalling them in wages, type of employment and geographical mobility during the eighteenth-month period. It was also thought that, after a period of working in a 'skilled' occupation, the trainees' attitudes and way of life would tend towards those exhibited by this group of craftsmen.

To get in touch with craftsmen, companies in areas from which the trainees had come and who might offer suitable employment for men trained at government training centres were approached and asked for their help in the research. The request made was for permission to interview several selected employees on company premises during working hours. The estimated disturbance time for each group was less than one hour and the company and men were promised confidentiality. Almost all companies approached were extremely helpful, and without their kind co-operation this work would not have been possible. The procedure used to interview and keep in touch with the craftsmen was the same as that used for the trainees. Of the 101 craftsmen interviewed initially, 96 completed final questionnaires (some after a personal interview), a response rate of 95.2 per cent.

Operators

Contact with men classed as 'operators' was made by approaching companies in the same way as for craftsmen. Personnel officers were asked to help in the selection of men who were doing jobs of a semi-skilled or un-skilled nature and which required not more than six weeks on-the-job training. These workers would hold jobs similar to those held by many of the trainees prior to training, and it was thought that they would help to monitor any changes in the life-style of trainees in the post-training period and provide a host of additional information.

With the help of the companies approached, 102 operators were interviewed and subsequently followed up in the usual manner. Completed final questionnaires were obtained for 96 of those men – a response rate of 94.1 per cent.

Unemployed

As over two-fifths (41.1 per cent) of the trainees had applied for government training when registering with an employment exchange, it was considered important to compare their fortunes with unemployed men who were considered suitable for training courses but who had elected not to take the opportunity. A control group of unemployed men would also give some indication of factors which prevented some such men from attending government training centres.

The staff of employment exchanges were asked to help in the selection of men who had been unemployed for a period of two months or more and who could benefit from government training centre courses. The period of two months was designed to exclude unemployment associated with normal job mobility. Despite this specification later follow-up showed that the unemployed sample were not, on the basis of a number of criteria, on a par with the trainees who were unemployed when applying for government training centres; yet they were as good a match as was possible under the circumstances.

Response was poorest from the group of 100 men contacted in this way as form-filling proved to be a difficult task for many of them. Eventually a response rate of 93.0 per cent was obtained after 43 men completed questionnaires with the help of an interviewer.

Apprentices

The group of final-year apprentices who were interviewed were important in forming another group of men who were reaching the end of a period of training and study at the same time as the trainees were finishing their courses. It was thought that when the apprentices completed their periods of indentured training and were free to move, their job and geographical mobility might in some ways resemble those of the trainees in the immediate post-training period, although there would be obvious differences between the two groups such as age and family responsibilities.

To contact apprentices, technical colleges were asked to provide facilities to interview final-year apprentices attending day-release classes. These apprentices may not have been entirely typical of the total apprentice population because of their continuing academic training throughout the whole of their apprenticeship period. However, they did serve the purposes of the enquiry extremely well as the end of supervised technical classes would emphasise the end of their training period.

The apprentices were the most loyal of all groups contacted and only 10 required to be interviewed at the end of the survey period. Replies were obtained from 101 of the original 103 men interviewed, making a response rate of 98.1 per cent. Unfortunately one questionnaire was returned from Australia too late to be included for data processing, so only 100 apprentices appear in the tables.

Our debt to all these men who so loyally filled in questionnaires and gave useful intimate details of their working lives must be apparent.

Chapter 6

The Pre-training Situation of the Longitudinal Sample of Trainees

The cyclical nature of employment opportunities has been a feature of postwar Britain and it may therefore be necessary, before studying the type of person who was attending government training centres in 1968–9, to consider the employment situation prevailing at that time. In late 1968 unemployment levels were not particularly high, although it was the beginning of the upward trend which approached the critical number of one million unemployed (4.3 per cent of the labour force) in early 1972; unemployment in Scotland at that time was even higher at 7.1 per cent of the labour force. The unemployment level for the nation in December 1968 was 2.4 per cent, the comparative Scottish figure was 3.6 per cent and there was little to suggest then that the unemployment situation would worsen and that it would produce an inhibiting effect on voluntary labour mobility. Possibly as a result of the relatively good situation in 1968, over half (58.9 per cent) of the trainees in this sample had been in regular employment prior to attending training centres.

The reasons why some unemployed persons should opt for training can be quite easily understood; they may simply attempt to make as much use as possible of the unfortunate situation in which they find themselves. However, it is important to realise that to attend a training centre is not the easiest solution to an individual's unemployment situation; it may be easier to remain with the employment exchange hoping to find a job offering on-the-job training or to continue in a pattern of short-term jobs offering limited prospects. If government training centre training is the obvious answer to unemployment then it would of course not have been possible to find the control group of unemployed men who were considered to be suitable for training yet had not taken advantage of the opportunity. These men were asked why they had not attempted a government training centre course. It was surprising to discover that 10 of the 93 men interviewed at employment exchanges (10.8 per cent) claimed that they did not know about government training courses; if these men were in fact suitable for retraining then the Department of Employment staff should have discussed with them the opportunities which training for a new skill would

70

offer; therefore the chances are that either the topic was never raised with them or was raised in a manner which made little impression. The fact is that 33 of the 83 men (39.8 per cent) who did know of the training schemes said that they just 'did not want to [train]' and 11 others (13.3 per cent) stated that no one had offered them training or that they did not know how to set about applying for training. The other indicator of inadequate information was the fact that 8 men (9.6 per cent) informed us that they would not be able to manage on the allowances paid during training. At that time training allowances were in fact slightly higher than unemployment benefits.[1] One assumption may be that when our unemployed men stated that they could not manage on the allowances they were unaware of the differences rather than that they were admitting that training would mean that they would have to miss possible illicit earnings from casual labouring jobs which would not be open to them if they were in a government training centre for forty hours a week; we have no factual information on this matter. Twenty-three other men offered a variety of reasons for not wanting to train, of which 8 were of special interest. These 8 men had avoided training because they felt that they had no more guarantee of regular employment after training than they did have while registering with the employment exchange. This is a difficult sentiment to contradict as, although training someone who has no employable skill to offer may increase his employability, there is certainly no guarantee that government training centre training will ensure regular employment or even easy entry into the pertinent labour market.

With this display of ignorance or ignoring of training facilities from the group of unemployed men it was interesting to speculate how the trainees who previously had been unemployed had overcome the factual or imaginary problems which had inhibited the 'unemployed' control group from volunteering for training. Unfortunately no data are available giving this group's reasons for training, so it is not possible to know this exactly. What is known is that the circumstances surrounding the trainees' unemployment differed from those of the men who were still registering at the employment exchange; this is illustrated in Table 6.1. Many of the 106 previously unemployed trainees had been precipitated into unemployment by factors outside their control such as illness (34.9 per cent) or redundancy (30.2 per cent), but only a quarter (26.9 per cent) of those 93 men still out of work were victims of these circumstances. This trainee sample contained a high number of men who had been made redundant following a colliery disaster in Fife and who had chosen to remain in their home areas and train for another job rather than to continue their mining career in pits in the north of England and elsewhere. This attitude of mining communities is hardly unique to Scotland. Few of the unemployed sample could be considered as 'victims of circumstances' when the variations assigned to

---

[1] Legislation in late 1971 made training allowances considerably higher than unemployment benefits. In an era of inflation the actual figures change frequently, but the differential has been maintained.

the word 'redundancy' were studied. Only 6 of the 22 redundant men interviewed at the employment exchange had been in their jobs long enough to be eligible for redundancy pay under the Redundancy Payments Act;[2] and most (68.8 per cent) of the 16 others had been employed in short-term construction contracts. In comparison only 2 of the 32 redundant trainees had not been in their last jobs for more than two years. In a similar way, 29 of the 106 trainees (27.4 per cent) left employment because of disagreements, dissatisfactions or sacking, compared with 58.1 per cent of the 93 unemployed men (p < .001).[3] From these figures it would appear that the men who leave the employment exchange to train represent a different and possibly more stable sector of the labour market than the men who decide not to take advantage of the training facilities offered.

TABLE 6.1 *Comparison of reasons for being unemployed for those men who were unemployed at time of application for training with those men who remained unemployed although considered suitable for retraining*

Reason	Trainees %	Unemployed %
Ill-health	34.9	3.2
Redundancy	30.2	23.7
Dissatisfied	13.2	22.6
Sacked	4.7	7.5
Disagreement/misconduct	9.4	28.0
In order to train	1.9	—
Personal	—	8.6
Others	3.8	4.3
Never worked	0.9	—
Don't know	0.9	2.2
TOTAL	99.9 (N = 106)	100.1 (N = 93)

Note: Throughout the chapter figures in italics in the tables indicate percentages.

Having considered the disdvantages of retraining as seen from the unemployed man's viewpoint it is easy to appreciate the reservations with which an unemployed man enters training. How much greater must be the misgivings of men who have to leave regular employment to embark on this doubtful future. Of the 152 men who left regular employment to attend training centres some were in a situation where their job tenure was in

[1] The Redundancy Payments Acts of 1965 and 1969, affecting these trainees, define a minimum period of 104 weeks of continuous employment with one employer in order to make a person eligible for financial compensation under the Act. We are not suggesting that if a person is thrown out of a job before the period of two years has elapsed because his job had disappeared he is not redundant – to do so would be both grotesque and unjust.

[3] Throughout the remainder of this text statistical significances will only be stated if they do not meet the minimum of p < .05 or better.

doubt, either because of imminent redundancy (12 men) or illness (15 men), but the remaining 116 men appeared to be true volunteers. All were asked to give their reasons for giving up regular work to start training and their answers are shown in Table 6.2. This shows both the number of times each reason was mentioned and the number of men who gave that as their only reason.

TABLE 6.2   *Reasons why men applying for training while in regular employ-ment should want a change*

Reason	Total no. of times mentioned	No. of men giving this as sole reason
Imminent redundancy	12 7.9	5
Insecurity	52 34.2	14
Low earnings	48 31.6	11
Low status	41 27.0	9
Irregular employment	9 5.9	1
Ill-health	15 9.9	10
Discharge from Forces	8 5.3	8
Home circumstances	8 5.3	8
Lack of advancement	9 5.9	6
Desire for skill	15 9.9	8
Others	18 11.8	10
No. of choices	235	90
No. of trainees (N)	152	

First of all it is noticeable that the 15 men who had been ill placed con-siderable emphasis on this; for two-thirds it was their only reason for attending a government training centre. However, the other group of men facing possible unemployment were those who were anticipating redun-dancy, yet 9 of the 21 affected by redundancy did not even mention this as a factor which motivated them in volunteering for training. This could suggest that they had been contemplating training for other reasons and the prospect of redundancy had merely precipitated the decision. Other reasons which were factual, relating to the man's actual rather than his perceived circumstances, were those given by the 8 men who had been discharged from the armed forces and 8 others whose home circumstances made them seek training. All the other men gave reasons which expressed dissatisfaction with their employment situation. The most frequently quoted reason was 'insecurity' followed closely by 'low earnings' and 'low status'; in fact these three reasons were closely linked, and of the 38 men who mentioned other reasons in addition to insecurity, 6 spoke of low earnings and low status and 22 others mentioned either low earnings (15 men) or low status (7 men). Not unexpectedly 9 of the 10 men who thought that their employment was irregular felt insecure. This preoccupation with lack of security in employment occurs again and is discussed below (p. 79).

THE IMAGE OF THE CRAFTSMAN

The foregoing appears to support the popular image of the craftsman as the elite of the manual work-force holding a job with high security, status, and earnings. (Craftsmen will dispute part of this picture as untrue and cite how the earnings of semi-skilled men creep up on and sometimes surpass their own, but they are far less likely to contradict the image of elitism.) This view of the craftsman appeared to be more common among those who had no personal experience of craft tradition than among those who had enjoyed a measure of apprenticeship training at some point. Eleven of the 86 men with no craft experience wanted a skill yet only 4 of the 66 who had experienced craft training desired this. It is possible that at least some of those who have seen the inside of the apprenticeship system and have been initiated into the 'mystery' of a craft see the status of a tradesman in a more realistic light than those who have been denied access for one reason or another.

The analysis of the above questions is an attempt to discover the motivation behind the behaviour of adults who either leave employment or because of unemployment choose to embark on a training course which offers an uncertain future at its end. The type of man who takes this gamble in employment is described below.

THE SAMPLE OF TRAINEES

We do not wish to exaggerate the Scottishness of the majority of our sample for the simple reason that our non-Scottish control group plus the work of the social survey (see footnote 3 in Chapter 1) indicate that in so far as this research project went, the similarities between the UK at large and the Scottish situation far exceed any dissimilarities, but it may be useful to discuss briefly the geographical disposition of the trainees. As was mentioned in Chapter 5, most of the trainees came from the east of Scotland and Table 6.3 shows that they were further concentrated in the Lothians and in Fife, the two areas in the east of Scotland where a training centre is within daily travelling distance. Although Angus contains the busy industrial region surrounding Dundee only a small proportion of trainees come from that part. This was not because of good alternative employment prospects; in December 1969 Dundee had an unemployment rate of 3.4 per cent (5 per cent for men). It might be suggested that the low numbers from this area were a result of the reluctance to live away from home during training and if this was the case the establishment of the new government training centre in Dundee should now have solved this problem. The numbers of trainees from the north-east of Scotland and from the Borders and other areas is in contrast to the numbers from Dundee and reflects the situation in areas where employment prospects are limited. There is a tradition of emigration from the north of Scotland to the more populous areas of the country; the recent oil boom may stem the flow but the oil finds off north Scotland were not an issue during the research period and in any case affect mainly the east coast.

TABLE 6.3   *Geographical distribution of trainees*

Area	% of trainees
Edinburgh and Lothians	36.8
East and West Fife	28.7
Angus	6.2
North-east Scotland	12.0
Others	16.3
TOTAL	100.0
	(N = 258)

The trainees ranged in age from 17 to 56 years with 47.2 per cent of the sample concentrated in the 21 to 30 age group (see Table 6.4). The ideal lower limit for entry to a government training centre is 20; to train men younger than this may result in someone of apprenticeship age seeking work normally held by craftsmen which may lead to problems with skilled men. The 7 trainees who were younger than 20 were either near enough their twentieth birthday not to become entangled in that difficult situation or had been involved in accidents which forced them to give up previous apprenticeship positions.

More than three-quarters (76.0 per cent) of the trainees were married and all but 29 of these 196 men had children. 66.3 per cent of the families had children under school-leaving age so that it may have been impossible for many of the wives to supplement the family income in any way during the training period, which does suggest that when the men were informed about the available training allowances most must have realised that these were at least at a level which would allow them to attend government training centres despite the responsibilities of having a young family to support – even though without doubt some suffered hardships.

The education received by most of the trainees had been the minimum possible. Almost exactly a quarter of them had received some further academic education or training beyond their basic general education; the standards they achieved were not high and only 8 of the 65 men involved had managed to get some 'O' levels. Of the 28 trainees who attended day-release or evening classes related to their previous employment only 6 had managed to gain certificates of any sort; 2 of these had gained City and Guilds certificates. Other training had been given by the Army (10 men) the Coal Board (8 men) or technical colleges (8 men). A similar proportion of operators (29.2 per cent) had received some form of further education but they tended to have more to show for it in the end; 10 of the 28 operators (35.7 per cent) who had undertaken further education had earned certificates compared to 14 (21.5 per cent) of the 65 trainees. However, the trainees were significantly better educated than the group of unemployed men as only 15.1 per cent of the latter enjoyed any form of further education. As might be imagined, vocational education was often related to previous employment and so to experience of the apprenticeship system. Among the trainees, 22 had completed apprenticeships, 86 had started off on apprenticeships but failed to complete these and the majority (150 men) had never started trade training.

TABLE 6.4   *Age distribution of trainees in Scotland*

Age	Numbers
Under 21	17
	6.6
21–30	122
	47.2
31–40	59
	22.9
41–50	54
	20.9
51 and over	6
	2.3
TOTAL	$N = 258$
	% = 99.9

Although many of the trainees did not have the opportunity of learning a trade when they left school, a large number had been offered the chance but had failed, for a variety of reasons, to make full use of it. Of the 108 men who had the opportunity to qualify as tradesmen, only 22 did so. More of the men over 40 (42.1 per cent) had completed their courses than the 'younger' (15.7 per cent) men. This difference might in part be accounted for by the traditional respect which older men have for trade training and by the wider employment opportunities which had been available to the younger men. The proportion of craftsmen in the trainee sample (8.8 per cent) is very similar to those among the unemployed group (9.7 per cent) but is significantly less than the numbers (16.7 per cent) in the group of operators.

Reasons for the craftsmen wishing to gain another trade at a government training centre must be difficult to understand, particularly if they hold the typical craft prejudices against these 'six-month wonders' from training centres. Of the 22 trainees with completed apprenticeships, 5 upgraded their skills with another training course. An RAF radio operator and an electrician (also in the RAF) became radio and television mechanics; this course might give them the skilled recognition in civilian life which the RAF course denied, which would explain their action. An engineering craftsman was becoming a draughtsman which was a job more suited to his unfortunate health record, and a radio and television mechanic was taking further study to upgrade himself to the level of an instrument mechanic. Of the other craftsmen, 5 men had skills which were now redundant, 7 men were suffering from ill health, 4 men from the food trades claimed they had lost interest, and 2 men had let their skill slide because of lack of practice.

The other men who were second time around at their attempt to gain a skill were asked why they had not completed their apprenticeships; their stated reasons are shown in Table 6.5. The most frequently quoted reason was 'joining the Forces', yet arrangements had been made for servicemen after demobilisation to complete apprenticeships interrupted by national service if they had failed to take advantage of the deferment offered them. For some of these at least, the reasons may be related to the second most popular reason given, that of finance; to earn as much money as his peers is more likely to be important to many a teenager than the process of acquiring a trade. If one adds to the above those 8 men who were forced to give up because of ill health, then the other reasons are in the main not untypical of the situation in which a youth does not enjoy the benefit of vocational guidance or home support.

TABLE 6.5 *Reasons given by trainees, operators and unemployed for not completing an apprenticeship*

Reason	Trainees	Operators	Unemployed
Financial	17	6	3
	19.8	*40.0*	*13.6*
Joining the Forces	25	1	10
	29.1	*6.7*	*45.5*
Loss of interest	12	5	3
	14.0	*33.3*	*13.6*
Ill-health	7	1	—
	8.1	*6.7*	—
Sacked	4	1	3
	4.7	*6.7*	*13.6*
Bad conditions	4	1	1
	4.7	*6.7*	*4.5*
Others	17	—	2
	19.8	—	*9.1*
TOTAL	N = 86	15	22
	% = *100.2*	*100.1*	*99.9*

That at least some young people do not obtain adequate career guidance when it would be most telling was made clear to us during our discussion with members of the various groups. This lack of guidance for young people is again illustrated when looking at the reasons why some men never started apprenticeships (see Table 6.6). The 37 men (24.7 per cent of those who never started apprenticeships) who claim they were 'not interested' or did not start because of their own ignorance of the value of apprenticeship training, point, at least in part, to the lack of adequate information on careers for school-leavers. A large number (34.7 per cent) of the 150 trainees were unable to get apprentice training either because of limited opportunities or because the area in which they lived did not offer many apprenticeships. When faced with situations like these, which have a lasting effect on the career of the man involved it would seem only sensible to offer such men a second chance to learn a manual skill should they so desire. The alternative to the second chance is to ensure that every school-leaver has access to proper vocational guidance and that he is given the required support to enable him to carry out his planned career. And yet, in an age of rapid technological change, the same difficulties may still be met when a man in his middle years, despite proper guidance and help in youth, finds his skill is redundant. It is important to offer this second chance if the country is to make the best use of its available manpower.

TABLE 6.6   *Reasons for not starting an apprenticeship given by trainees, operators and unemployed*

Reason	Trainees %	Operators %	Unemployed %
Could not get one	34.7	33.8	19.4
Not interested	22.0	30.8	33.9
Joined the Forces	10.7	1.5	8.1
Finance	5.3	10.8	17.7
Ignorance	2.7	—	1.6
Others	16.0	23.1	16.1
Reason not given	8.7	—	3.2
TOTAL N =	150	65	62
% =	100.1	100.0	100.0

The foregoing gives a picture of our Mr Average Trainee as a man in his early thirties, married with children aged under 15. There is a 50-50 chance that he has already had the opportunity to learn a skill by starting an apprenticeship but he abandoned this at some point. He may have given up regular employment to embark on a training course; there is a slightly smaller possibility that he was unemployed at the time of his application.

THE TRAINEES' HOPES AND EXPECTATIONS

One thing which has still to be examined is the hopes which these trainees held for the outcome of their training. All were asked to choose from a list of seven factors (selected after the pilot survey) those which were important to them in reaching the decision to train. If they wished to choose more than one reason they were asked to rank all reasons up to four in number; space was left for the men to include other reasons not mentioned. Table 6.7 shows the results for all trainees excluding just one who omitted this question.

Once again high numbers of men were looking for 'more security' and linked this to the hunt for 'more money'; 83.9 per cent who wanted security also wanted more money while only 47.2 per cent of the 52 trainees who made no mention of job security sought a higher income. Table 6.8 shows that both groups give job satisfaction and mobility importance but there are differences in the significance attached to status. Of those 205 men who sought security, 34.1 per cent also wanted higher status, but only 11.3 per cent of the other 52 men thought it important.

TABLE 6.7   *Factors which influenced the Scottish trainees' decisions to attend government training centres*

Factor	First choice	Second choice	Third choice	Fourth choice	Total
More security	113	44	27	21	205 *79.8*
More money	36	103	48	10	197 *76.7*
More satisfying job	77	54	51	21	203 *79.0*
Higher social status	4	9	27	36	76 *29.6*
Able to move elsewhere in Scotland	1	5	19	15	40 *15.6*
Able to move elsewhere in the UK	7	10	20	40	77 *30.0*
Able to move overseas	1	—	3	3	7 *2.7*
To avoid moving	7	10	11	19	47 *18.3*
Ill-health	10	1	3	1	15 *5.8*
Others	1	3	1	4	9 *3.5*

Note: Figures in italics express total number of trainees choosing each factor as a percentage of the total number of trainees answering this question (N = 257).

Table 6.2 indicated that the general feeling of insecurity acted as a powerful stimulus for seeking a change. This importance of security varied according to the age of the trainee, as Table 6.9 indicates. However, it was not only the older trainees with their pre-war memories who had this desire for security – the younger men in fact voiced this desire more strongly than their older compatriots; 83.3 per cent of the 198 men aged under 40 wanted security compared with 63.3 per cent of the men aged over 40. Fewer of the older men wanted to move than their younger colleagues and more had trained specifically to avoid moving. Ill-health was also a more important factor for the older men.

TABLE 6.8   *Importance of other factors influencing decision to train on those who wanted more security and those who made no mention of security*

Factor	Those who wanted more security %	Those who made no mention of security %
More money	83.9	47.2
More job satisfaction	80.0	73.6
Able to move [a]	46.8	52.8
Higher social status	34.1	11.3
To avoid moving	19.5	13.2
Ill-health	2.4	18.9
Others	2.4	7.5
	N = 205	52

[a] In this table the three choices, 'able to move elsewhere in Scotland', 'able to move elsewhere in the UK' and 'able to move overseas' shown in Table 6.7 have been combined to give 'able to move'.

This preoccupation with feelings of insecurity in employment has appeared in many surveys of factors important in job satisfaction [4] and has been discussed in relation to this sample elsewhere.[5] Richard Centers [6] claims that the desire for security is characteristic of the working class and that those who have experienced unemployment need security; it is only when men are in better economic circumstances that they become emancipated 'from such a basic need'. Neither of the above points can be supported by this survey. Firstly, although most of the trainees would be assigned to the working class by the status of their training occupation, their ranking of themselves on the class scale ranged from middle class to lower working class.[7] There were no significant differences in the numbers of men seeking security among those who graded themselves in the middle, lower middle or upper working classes (78.8 per cent) and those who graded

[4] R. M. Jones, 'A Case Study in Labour Mobility', *The Manchester School of Economic and Social Studies*, Vol. 37, No. 2, June 1969.

[5] K. Hall and L. Miller, 'Supplying Skills the Government Way', *Personnel Management* (April 1970).

[6] R. Centers, *The Psychology of Social Classes* (Princeton University Press, 1949).

[7] This will be discussed in Chapter 10.

TABLE 6.9   *Factors which influenced 'older' and 'younger' trainees in
their decision to attend a government training centre*

Factor	Under 40	Over 40	Total
More security	165	40	205
	83.3	*63.3*	
More money	164	33	197
	82.8	*55.0*	
More job satisfaction	164	39	203
	82.8	*65.0*	
Higher social status	66	10	76
	33.3	*16.7*	
Able to move [a]	100	24	124
	50.5	*40.0*	
To avoid moving	31	16	47
	15.7	*26.7*	
Ill-health	5	10	15
	2.5	*16.7*	
Others	8	1	9
	4.0	*1.7*	
	N = 198	59	

Note: Figures in italics express number of trainees who chose each factor as a
percentage of the total number of trainees in each group. Percentages
amount to more than 100 per cent because each trainee could choose up to
four factors which influenced him.

[a] In this table the three choices 'able to move elsewhere in Scotland',
'able to move elsewhere in UK' and 'able to move overseas' shown
in Table 6.7 have been combined to give 'able to move'.

themselves as working or lower working class (79.6 per cent). Secondly,
there were no significant differences between the numbers seeking security
among those men who were unemployed prior to attending government
training centres (74.5 per cent of the 106 men) and others (82.9 per cent of
the 152 who were employed). At the time of the survey no satisfactory
solution could be forwarded as to why there was such a high demand for
security, as employment was not threatened in the way it was during the
period 1971–2. Even now one can only make the tentative assumption that
the men who sought security were possibly aware of the hazardous situation of their employment where they formed part of a semi-skilled labour
force which, if threatened with unemployment, had no transferable skill
to offer. And possibly security is a generic term to cover general dissatisfaction with the work situation and/or work prospects. This is in part supported by the consistency with which low earnings and low status are
allied with desire for security (see Table 6.9). It is enough to say that an
analysis of the post-training employment histories of these trainees shows

that to begin a government training centre course hoping that it will bring a fully secure future is for many simply false optimism.

If this group had not been successful in being accepted for government training centre courses in order to fulfil these ambitions, 68.2 per cent of the men, according to their claim, would have taken some action to improve their employment prospects. The most favoured ways of improving their status would have been to hunt for a better job or to take some form of additional education which would lead to the same type of prospects as government training centres were seen to offer. Their determination may be contrasted to the group of operators working in semi-skilled employment of whom 49 men, i.e. 51.0 per cent, did not want the opportunity to train for a higher skill and only 28 per cent had ever taken any action which might have helped to upgrade them or improve their prospects. Obviously, the majority of the two different groups operate within differing frames of reference; it is not for us to suggest that one is preferable to the other.

This brief sketch of the motivation behind the trainees' decision to train shows the significance which the men were placing on this major career change. Their success in realising their ambitions is described elsewhere.

Chapter 7

The Training of a Group of Government Training Centre Trainees – Their Views on the Training and Their Post-training Labour Market Experience

INTRODUCTION

The training given at government training centres, in spite of the short training time and limited shop-floor experience, is generally recognised as being of a high calibre. Before the establishment of industrial training boards many time-served craftsmen could not claim to have had such good instruction and even now the standards of apprenticeship training vary greatly. On the other hand accelerated training courses cannot hope to cover every aspect of a trade in depth nor can a trainee achieve the practice and skill of the craftsman who has four years or so in which to absorb and apply his knowledge. It remains to be seen whether a properly organised training course crammed into a short period can compensate for the more leisurely training of an apprenticeship which may have rather haphazard instruction, and whether these accelerated courses can from the start sufficiently equip adults for efficient employment in skilled jobs. The other difference in the two types of trade training is that the pupils attending accelerated courses are adults whose learning facility may be rusty and therefore not as sharp as that of a teenager. However, the adult may have the advantage of more serious application to his task of learning than the youth apprentice who, if he resembles the trainees in this sample and the reasons they gave for dropping out of apprenticeships, may not understand the importance of the training which they receive. Also, the work of Dr Eunice Belbin and her associates [1] has shown that, provided instruction is given to adults in an appropriate manner, then age is no barrier to learning new skills in a relatively short time.

The best judges of the degree of success which the training can achieve

[1] E. Belbin, 'Adult Training and Retraining', *Industrial Training International* (August 1967).

are the trainees themselves, and for evaluation of government training centres their comments and criticisms must therefore be carefully studied.

One of the first tests of training is the numbers of people who can successfully find jobs using their trade. The trainees in this longitudinal research project formed three different employment groups as follows: Group A involving 177 men (68.6 per cent) who used their trade in every job held after training; Group B with 52 men (20.2 per cent) who used their training in at least one job after leaving government training centres but who also held other 'unskilled' jobs; and Group C which consisted of 29 men (11.2 per cent) who were unable to use their skill in any post-training job. The relatively large numbers in Group A may be perceived as a tribute to the training. The fact that 68.6 per cent of the sample were able to successfully change their employment and to embark on a new career where they had for the whole of the eighteen-month period continually used their skill justifies the efforts which have made the government training centres a feature of industrial society which is steadily growing in importance.[2]

THE QUALITY OF TRAINING

The general feeling among the trainees was that the standard of training had been good or at least adequate for the type of employment they had obtained. At the end of the eighteen-month period they were asked to rate their training on a scale ranging from 'very good' to 'poor' (see Table 7.1). Most of the trainees felt that their training had been 'very good' (32.9 per cent) or 'good' (32.9 per cent); a further 56 men said it had been 'adequate' (21.7 per cent) and only 28 men stated that it had been 'poor' (10.9 per cent).

TABLE 7.1   *Comparison of opinion of training with employment success for those who used their skill throughout the 18-month period (A), those who used their skill some of the time (B), and those who never used their skill (C)*

Rating	A %	B %	C %	Total %
Very good	*39.0*	*19.2*	*20.7*	*32.9*
Good	*32.2*	*34.6*	*34.5*	*32.9*
Adequate	*22.6*	*23.1*	*13.8*	*21.7*
Poor	*5.6*	*19.2*	*27.6*	*10.9*
Don't know	*0.6*	*3.8*	*3.4*	*1.6*
TOTAL	% = *100.0* N = 177	*99.9* 52	*100.0* 29	*100.0* 258

Note: Throughout the chapter figures in italics in the tables indicate percentages.

[2] A later study by the authors and Miss Christine Denholm indicated that over 60 per cent of a sample of government training centre trainees in Scotland were still using their training skills five years or more after the completion of their training courses – this at a time of high unemployment, which may be seen as a vindication of the concept of government training of adults, and of liberal trade union attitudes (see Chapter 11).

As might be imagined, the opinion of training depended on the success which the trainee had in using his skill. It will be noted that of the successful group A, 39.0 per cent rated their training as 'very good' (the highest rating), compared with 19.2 per cent of group B, and 20.7 per cent of group C. However, despite these differences more than half the men in groups B and C still thought that their training ranked as 'good' or 'very good'. In group C, 27.6 per cent wrote their training off as 'poor' with only 13.8 per cent prepared to rate the instruction under the non-critical term of 'adequate'.

The judgements on training show a clear relationship to the trainees' employment situation at the time of answering their questionnaires. At the end of the eighteen months, 69 trainees were not using their skill, 14 were unemployed and the remaining 175 were in 'skilled' employment (see Table 7.2). The training was 'very good' according to 38.3 per cent of those using their skill and 23.2 per cent of those who were employed but not using their skill, a difference which is significant at the 5 per cent level.

TABLE 7.2   *Comparison of opinion of training and employment situation at the end of the survey period*

Rating	Using skill %	Not using skill %	Unemployed %	Total %
Very good	38.3	23.2	14.3	32.9
Good	33.1	31.9	35.7	32.9
Adequate	22.3	18.8	28.6	21.7
Poor	5.7	21.7	21.4	10.9
Don't know	0.6	4.3	—	1.6
TOTAL % =	100.0	99.9	100.0	100.0
N =	175	69	14	258

According to Belbin [3] learning becomes more difficult with age, so that one would expect the 'older' men of over 40, given a more difficult situation, to have a poorer view of training than the younger men. In fact this is not the case: 31.8 per cent of the younger trainees thought their training 'very good' compared with 36.7 per cent of the older men. As the older men contain more of the critical group who never used their skills after training, the reverse of the expected situation becomes apparent if the reactions of only the successful men are studied. Fewer (36.1 per cent) of the young successful trainees had a very high opinion of their training than the old successful trainees, 53.3 per cent of whom thought that their training had been 'very good'. This difference is, however, only significant at the 10 per cent level. It may be that the older men tended to blame

[3] E. Belbin, 'Training the Adult Worker', *Problems of Progress in Industry*, No. 15 (HMSO, 1964).

their failure on their age and their inadequacies rather than on the training.

That the training trade [4] made quite a difference to the opinions of the

TABLE 7.3   *Opinion of training compared with training trade*

Rating	Construction %	Engineering %	Motor repair %	Others %	Total %
Very good	22.0	42.2	14.7	37.5	32.9
Good	35.6	30.3	38.2	32.1	32.9
Adequate	25.4	17.4	32.4	19.6	21.7
Poor	15.3	7.3	14.7	10.7	10.9
Don't know	1.7	2.8	—	—	1.6
TOTAL % =	100.0	100.0	100.0	99.9	100.0
N =	59	109	34	56	258

quality of their training as held by the trainees is shown by Table 7.3. It will be noticed that construction trainees (joiners and bricklayers) and vehicle repair trainees were more critical than others. The difference between the 22.0 per cent of construction workers and the 36.2 per cent of all other trainees who rated their training as 'very good' should be noted. The construction trainees were the first to feel the effects of the unemployment slump of the late 1960s and early 1970s and their reactions possibly reflect their difficulties in obtaining suitable work and in competing with the increasing numbers of skilled craftsmen who were also seeking work. Both bricklayers and joiners were equally critical. The other group of critical trainees were in the motor vehicle repair trades but here they grouped themselves according to which particular trade within the motor industry they had studied. Of the 11 motor mechanics, 8 thought their training had been 'very good' but none of the 6 heavy vehicle repair trainees were able to rate their training higher than 'adequate'. The 17 agricultural fitting trainees were not too enthusiastic either. These criticisms may be related to labour market factors; the motor mechanics had employment problems (see Chapter 8) but they did know in which area of employment they were competing, whilst the heavy vehicle repair mechanics did not have such a clearly defined position. This rating according to the labour market situation is repeated with the radio and television mechanics as all of the 15 men who trained in this trade, and were able to obtain work with little difficulty, thought that their training had been 'good' or 'very good'. So it would appear that opinion and labour market experience are linked, although of course some other variable, such as acceptance by work-mates or employers, cannot be ignored.

Although the trainees could rate their training highly, some still felt that it was inadequate for the first jobs which they held after leaving their respective government training centres. Those men who rated their train-

[4] For a full list of training trades see Table 8.4, p. 95.

ing as 'very good' eighteen months after the end of their courses made, in general, few criticisms when they wrote in after their first six months on the labour market. The main dissatisfaction which they expressed was not with their training but the lack of opportunity to use it; they wanted the training centres to give them more help in finding suitable jobs. The level of satisfaction at the end of the survey correlates with the level shown after the initial experiences and does indicate that perhaps the comments should be carefully considered in planning any changes to the training courses.

The trainees were asked if they had any comments to make on their training and additional to this many volunteered information on how the courses might be improved. These comments did not mean that the trainees who made them felt that their training had been inadequate, but rather that the comments were often made by those who rated their course quite highly and yet felt that the course could be further improved if attention was paid to some particular point. The comments received during the survey could be ranged into various categories as Table 7.4 shows.

TABLE 7.4   *List of comments on training made by trainees*

Comment	No. of times mentioned
More practical experience	44
More placement help	29
Course should be longer	26
More up to date	14
More negotiation with unions	12
More theory	10
Specific points	13
Other comments	24

THE POST-TRAINING SITUATION

The most pressing requirement was to have more practical experience. This is a difficult requirement to meet because government training centres do not aim really to provide experience but only to instruct in the basic principles of each trade. To provide experience would make the courses longer and not necessarily better suited to the trainees' purpose, as much of the 'experience' really needed is experience pertaining to the particular firm in which the particular trainee is to be employed. This is often the case with engineering trades and to a lesser extent in the construction trades. The solution might be to extend the number of 'improver' courses similar to those already arranged for construction trainees and agricultural fitters. Trainees in these courses are not regarded as being fully skilled upon completing their government training centre course but have sixty weeks to reach this standard. Until that time is over the construction trainees are paid a percentage of the skilled rate, starting at 85 per cent and increasing to 100 per cent at the end of sixty weeks and the employer receives a small grant from the Department of Employment for his part in

the training. The agricultural fitting trainees are also given sixty weeks'
'continued training', but here the trainee is paid a training allowance from
the Department of Employment for the first ten weeks of his employment.
This latter arrangement was not widely used by the trainees in this group;
only 2 of the 17 agricultural fitters came under this scheme and both left
their first employment within six weeks so it certainly did not function
very well in this instance. The system of being paid a fixed allowance does
not relate to the trainee's work nor does it necessarily bear any relation to
the wages of the men with whom he works, so the percentage wage system
of the construction workers would seem to be more satisfactory. Although
the 'continued training' for construction workers would seem to be the
answer to the plea for 'more practical experience' this arrangement would
appear to have its limitations because job mobility among construction
trainees was high and few stayed with one employer during the full sixty-
week period. Some sort of arrangement is necessary for trainees to gain
practical experience and negotiations should continue between the Department of Employment, employers and unions to come to some working
arrangement.

Related to the complaint of 'more practical experience' is the suggestion
that the courses should be longer. Provided the trainees were not expected
to be super-craftsmen the day they left the training centre but could enter
the labour market more gently under supervised on-the-job training, this
demand for a longer course might be lessened. The motor vehicle trades,
in particular, seem to suffer greatly from the problems of a large amount
of theory to be absorbed in a short period and little opportunity to experience a great amount of fault-finding. The high diagnostic content of a
mechanic's job is a skill which cannot be learnt in the classroom alone,
but is acquired only after extensive work experience. One of the trainees
explained the problem in his own way: that he did not think that the
trainee 'got enough experience on cars, on fault-finding, and repairs, to
allow him to have confidence in his own decisions' and explained that he
was therefore at first a poor employment prospect because 'as garages have
set time for jobs and as labour and material charges are high, speed and
confidence are at a premium'. At present the motor mechanic trainees are
given semi-skilled status by their trade union for the first year of their
employment, but no arrangement is made to supervise their training or to
gear their wages to a more suitable rate. It ought to be possible to extend
the present arrangements to cover a proper scheme of continued training
which would give the trainee the experience which he requires.

Better arrangements for hiring trainees with due regard to their limitations would also help to alleviate the third problem, that of 'more placement help'. The numbers of men placed in skilled employment immediately
after leaving their training centre were higher where arrangements for 'continued training' existed, and later discussion (see Chapter 8) shows that
success in using the requisite training trade is to some extent dependent
upon the trainees' finding suitable work quickly. If the placement officer

at the training centre cannot arrange suitable employment for his trainees with companies who realise the limitations of these newly-trained men then it does seem unlikely that either the local employment exchange or the man on his own will have more success. For his first post-training job it is unlikely that a trainee will be able to get work without his employer knowing of his training background, as his lack of experience would soon find him out. It would appear better that he be accepted as a novice than for him to fight a losing battle in competition with fully skilled men. The pattern which seemed to emerge from this research was that once a trainee had gained sufficient on-the-job experience he was likely to move to his second job where, keeping his training background secret, he attempted to be accepted as a tradesman; this would avoid any possible ill-feeling from his fellow workers. Certain geographical areas would seem to require much more placement help than others. There was a tendency for trainees in the Edinburgh area and Angus to find work quickly; trainees from the north-east were also successful although the jobs they found were often not in their home areas. The difficult areas were Fife and the Borders, which are areas with known employment problems. The placement officers from the training centres provided figures of the numbers of trainees they had placed in suitable employment; these figures related closely to experiences of our trainees in different areas; for example, Dunfermline Government Training Centre in Fife had the lowest placement rate. It is difficult to know for certain that if more resources were put into placing trainees in areas with limited employment opportunities whether or not the success rates in these locations might be improved. And of course the general employment situation is significant: placement officers who had difficulties in the slump conditions of 1971–2 had a heyday during the brief 1973 boom.

Other comments which were received were much more specifically related to the content of the training courses. The fourteen comments that the courses should be more up to date came mainly from the nine typewriter mechanics who were often expected to repair not just typewriters (which were mostly electric) but business machines also. The facilities of this course lacked the hardware necessary to give the trainees an overall picture of the type of office machinery which they might have to repair.

Some of the comments were contradictory. Among the electronic wiremen, some ended up in more technical jobs than those for which they had been trained, and others were doing jobs limited to wiring only. The first group wanted more theory and the second group less. This is an example of a course that requires to define its market more carefully: does it aim to provide test technicians or does it aim to supply wiremen? The electronics industry in normal times always complains of shortages of technical staff but can itself offer short on-the-job training courses in limited wiring tasks.

The last problem was not related to the training content of the courses but was a request that the government training centres should establish better relations with the relevant unions. This comment may seem irrelevant and out of place when the negotiations between unions and the Department of Employment staff at national level governing arrangements for training adults are considered. However, if one considers how little the national executive of the unions may represent the feelings of their members on this issue and the lack of involvement of local trade union officials in their neighbouring government training centres (see Chapter 9) then the comments become very relevant. Some local officials were not prepared to take advantage of the invitation open to them to visit centres, to meet potential trainees and hence union recruits, and to explain union policy on membership for adult trainees. Let it be noted that in some other areas trade union officials are very active, partaking more regularly in the selection process of intending trainees and recruiting vigorously.

Despite these varying comments and suggestions from the trainees the general consensus was that the training was overall good or very good. The criticisms referred to the difficulties which the trainees met when job hunting and when they were employed and often related to the difficulty which is implicit in the definition of accelerated vocational training – the lack of experience.

Chapter 8

The First Eighteen Months after Training

SUCCESS AND FAILURE AFTER TRAINING

After spending six or twelve months learning a new trade the most important factor upon leaving the training centre was simply whether a man is able to find a job where he could make use of his recently acquired skill and how quickly he can begin work. Table 8.1 shows how long it took men to find jobs and what sort of work they managed to get.

TABLE 8.1 *Period of unemployment prior to first job according to type of job gained*

	Using skill %	Not using skill %	Total %
None	*70.9*	*21.6*	*63.6*
Less than 5 weeks	*17.7*	*16.2*	*17.4*
5–26 weeks	*10.5*	*48.6*	*15.9*
More than 26 weeks	*0.9*	*13.5*	*2.7*
Still unemployed	—	—	*0.4*
TOTAL	N = 220	37	258
	% = *100.0*	*99.9*	*100.0*

Note: Throughout the chapter figures in italics in the tables indicate percentages.

Almost two-thirds (63.6 per cent) of the sample started work with no delay and within five weeks of leaving training centres only about one in five were still without work. For some men a delay of two or three weeks may have been deliberate in that they may have been taking a well-earned holiday before returning to regular employment. Others, who lived outside the area immediately surrounding the training centre, needed a week or two in which to return home and investigate local work opportunities, as it was often difficult for training centre placement officers to find jobs outside their own parishes.

When the types of jobs which the men found are studied, it is disturbing to see the number of men who went directly into employment which did not make any use of their training. Fourteen men (5.4 per cent) entered 'unskilled' employment within five weeks of leaving government training

91

centres. For reasons which we did not fully establish these men appeared to have either consciously decided not to use their new skill or been forced by circumstances to forgo its utilisation upon completion of their training. For those who made the conscious decision, one wonders why they decided to complete training and not to leave earlier. Yet the fact that they did stick the course till the end suggests that these men may have envisaged this first job as a temporary one and hoped to find more suitable work at a later date. Ten of these fourteen men who took 'unskilled' jobs soon after the end of their courses did in fact use their training in later employment, so the 'wastage' here (from the Government's point of view) was minimal.

One significant factor which appears in Table 8.1 is the drop-off in the number of those who obtained suitable employment after five weeks or more without work. Of the 209 men who had little or no unemployment 93.3 per cent used their skill but only 51.0 per cent of those 49 men with more than five weeks' unemployment found 'suitable' work, a difference which is statistically highly significant. This difference does suggest that unless work can be found quickly there is a real danger that the men will never use their skills. If this is the case then it points to difficulties of training people in periods of high unemployment; unless the trainees can practise the recently learned theory then training may be of limited use. The factors operating here are obvious; as the period of unemployment lengthens the trainees lose confidence in their ability to use the skills they have mastered. Their training is a 'crash course' which is designed to cover the basic requirements of a trade and not much time can be spent on practice and the building up of speed and stamina. Also during unemployment the desire to find work of any description becomes more pressing and trainees may settle for any job which they can find. Inevitably, too, greater resistance to 'dilution' should be expected at times when the jobs of the time-served men themselves are at risk. It may not be too strong a suggestion to state that trade unions would be failing in their duty if they did not protect the interest of their existing members. The onus is by and large on our national decision-makers to keep unemployment down, if government training is to succeed.

The experience of longer periods of unemployment was related to the age of the trainee, and the location of his home. It was the 'older' trainee, aged over 40, who had difficulty in finding work, as Table 8.2 shows. Of the young trainees, 69.2 per cent found work immediately compared with 45.0 per cent of the men aged over forty. Although theory suggests that men will require to be trained or retrained in mid-life as the skills they learnt when young become redundant, it would appear that the prospects for men in middle age will be bleak unless the prejudices of employers towards hiring older men can be broken down. Once again, the state of the employment market could be crucial.

The ease with which the trainees found work varied according to the area in which they were looking for work. Men from the Lothians and from Angus found work quickly as did men whose homes were in the north-east of Scotland, but in many cases men from the latter area did not restrict their job hunting to their local district.[1] The areas where the men had difficulty getting work were those which have suffered from lack of employment opportunities, Fife and the Borders; only 53.8 per cent of the men from these areas had no unemployment compared with 45.5 per cent of men from other areas (a difference, however, which is not statistically significant). One would expect a similar situation to exist in other parts of the UK.

TABLE 8.2   *Period of unemployment prior to first job related to age*

	Under 40 %	Over 40 %	Total %
None	69.2	45.0	63.6
Less than 5 weeks	16.7	20.0	17.4
5–26 weeks	12.6	26.7	15.9
More than 26 weeks	1.0	8.3	2.7
Still unemployed	0.5	—	0.4
TOTAL N =	198	60	258
% =	100.0	100.0	100.0

Placement officers from the six training centres in Scotland provided figures showing the number of men they had placed in suitable employment and these relate closely to the experiences of trainees in the different areas. For example, Dunfermline Government Training Centre, which took trainees mainly from Fife, an area of high unemployment, had the lowest placement rate. Whether these placement figures could be improved by more resources put into placing trainees or whether it is simply the misfortune of centres in areas of high unemployment to have fewer trained men using their skills is yet to be examined.

Despite the periods of unemployment suffered by some men, eventually 203 men found jobs where they were using their skill, another 18 were in jobs which made 'partial' use of their training, i.e. although the trainees did not make full use of their training, these jobs would not have been open to them prior to training. Considerable job mobility occurred after this first stage so that to arrive at a definition of 'success' following training, it was decided to consider as successful those men who, throughout the eighteen months, were in jobs which made either complete or very significant use of their training (group A). The rest of the sample was divided into those men who used their skill in some jobs but not in others (group B) and those who never used their skill at all (group C). The composition of these groups depended again upon age and geographical location and also training trade.

First of all there is a marked difference between the under-40s and the over-40s in using their skill, as Table 8.3 illustrates. The difference between

[1] It should be noted that the research period preceded the Scottish oil boom which has changed the employment situation in the north-east.

the 50 per cent of the 60 men over 40 and the 74.2 per cent of the 198 younger men who always used their skill is significant at the 0.1 per cent level. The same difference is apparent at the other end of the scale where 25.0 per cent of the older men never used their skill compared with 7.1 per cent of the younger men. These findings tend to threaten the popular view that training or retraining is one of the answers to the employment problems of the older age group, which was quoted to us time and again by differing sectors of the industrial community. It must be asked if it is economically sensible to train older men when only half the number trained have the chance to establish themselves in their new trade. The risk of a training programme is a justifiable one for the men who are successful, but, for the others, lack of success following their training may be the psychological last straw for the men who feel discarded because of their age. As many as one-quarter (25.8 per cent) of the younger men failed to settle in their training trades, but they still have age on their side, and in any case a few may still have succeeded after the completion of the eighteen months' study period.

The relationship between job success and location is very similar to that between unemployment and location. The geographical areas where men suffered high initial unemployment, Fife and the Borders, were those in which fewer trainees established themselves successfully in new jobs. Only 56.3 per cent of trainees in Fife and the Border areas always used their training in employment, compared with 74.2 per cent of men from other areas.

TABLE 8.3   *Comparison with age of those who used their skill all of the time (A), those who used their skill some of the time (B), and those who never used their skill (C)*

	A %	B %	C %	Total %
Under 40	74.2	18.7	7.1	100.0
Over 40	50.0	25.0	25.0	100.0
TOTAL N = 177	52	29	258
% = 68.6	20.2	11.2	100.0

Small sample sizes make comparisons between trades impossible but Table 8.4 gives some indication of the success of different trades. The proportions using their skill in each of the trade groups does not differ greatly but the distribution of individual trades varies considerably.

The trades which did better than average were radio and television repair, instrument maintenance, centre-lathe turning, milling, welding and joinery. The outstanding success of the television repairmen may be attributed to several factors. Firstly, as a trade which has arisen from modern technology there is no tradition-based apprenticeship scheme with which the trainees must compete – in fact, the youth training schemes in this trade do not supply sufficient numbers of tradesmen so that the government trainees are meeting an obvious requirement for trained men and the pertinent trade union is glad to take on any men who wish to join. Secondly, the twelve-month training course is one demanding more ability than most of the other courses and selection for this course is quite strict. The same

TABLE 8.4   *Comparison of trades of trainees who used their skill all the time (A), those who used their skill some of the time (B), and those who never used their skill (C)*

	A	B	C	Total
Joinery	35	10	1	46
Bricklaying	9	2	2	13
TOTAL Construction trades	44	12	3	59
Grinding	5	6	5	16
Welding	21	5	1	27
Capstan setting/operating	18	9	5	32
Centre-lathe turning	15	1	1	17
Milling	12	2	—	14
Fitting	1	—	—	1
Draughtsmanship	2	—	—	2
TOTAL Engineering trades	74	23	12	109
Motor vehicle repair	8	3	—	11
Agricultural fitting	9	4	4	17
Heavy vehicle repair	4	2	—	6
TOTAL Motor repair trades	21	9	4	34
Radio and television repair	15	—	—	15
Watch and clock repair	1	1	4	6
Instrument maintenance	8	1	—	9
Electronic wiring	7	4	3	14
Typewriter repair	6	1	2	9
Hairdressing	1	1	1	3
TOTAL Miscellaneous trades	38	8	10	56
TOTAL SAMPLE	N = 177	52	29	258

factors operate for the course on instrument maintenance except that trainees from this course do not have such a wide variety of jobs to choose from; every town has its television repair service, but it is usually only the large continuous process plants, such as chemical works or breweries, which have need of instrument maintenance personnel.

The success of the turners and millers is more difficult to explain. Centre-lathe turning is still regarded as the stronghold of the craftsman and any dilution of this trade is very much frowned upon. However, employers appeared to have sufficient requirement for this type of person to be able to disregard union pressure where it manifested itself. The welders found themselves in an awkward position; one union regards welding as a trade, another rates it as semi-skilled. These trainees did not all remain as semi-skilled workers, but in some cases managed to penetrate the bastions of the craft union and wangle themselves membership illegally. The joiners are the last of the highly successful groups. If the research had covered twenty-four months instead of eighteen and had penetrated the slump period in the construction industry which then occurred it is possible that more men would have been found in group B which by the end of the research period was steadily growing as men found it more and more difficult to find jobs. The success of the construction trainees in establishing themselves even in such circumstances suggests that they would have benefited by the increased construction activity in 1973. Unfortunately it was not possible to evaluate how well the trainees compared with traditionally trained craftsmen in weathering the fluctuations of their industry.

At the other end of the spectrum were the men who had considerable difficulty in finding skilled work. They were trained in the following trades: watch and clock repairing, hairdressing, grinding, agricultural fitting, typewriter repairing and electronic wiring. In each of these trades more than 20 per cent of the trainees never used their training. Watch and clock repairing and hairdressing are two courses which have often been used for the training of disabled persons and they carry with them the associated difficulties of finding employment for anyone less than able-bodied. More important, the age of the small shop carrying out watch repairs has now virtually ended, much of this work being now carried out in factory workshops. Unless a man was fortunate enough to come from an area near a clock factory, or was prepared to move to such an area, making a living from this work was unlikely as he would not be sufficiently experienced to set up on his own. Hairdressing was a problem also, partly because of the craft-pride exhibited by many salons which wished to train their own operators, and partly because of the slump in traditional hairstyling. Also the pittance which hairdressers earn was a problem because, unless they can build up a clientele who are prepared to supplement the men's basic income by generous tipping, this job is not economically viable. Most of the trades described above would, given the additional problems which 'retraining' pose, make interesting case studies in the sociology of occupations – but that is beyond the scope of this book.

Grinding and agricultural fitting both compete with apprenticeship schemes and although it is not easy to explain the difficulties which the grinders experienced (particularly when compared with the successful turners), in the case of agricultural fitters lack of job opportunities was the main reason for the failure of men trained in that trade. Typewriter repairing has no apprenticeship and each manufacturer trains his own staff; this produces difficulties for the trainees who have no close experience of the machines of one particular manufacturer but have worked with a wide variety of machines. Their other problem was that they were unable to tackle all the different makes of business machines, as was expected of them. The problem of the electronic wiremen was that they seemed to fall between two industrial job categories as has previously been explained, in that they were too highly trained for simple wiring assembly jobs, yet not sufficiently trained for the more skilled tasks of a test technician.

During the eighteen-month study period trainees took some time to settle down and changed jobs quite a lot. Less than one-half (43.8 per cent) stayed in the same job throughout the study period. Sixty-six men changed jobs once, 41 men moved twice, and 37 men were more mobile, with 4 or more jobs. Mobility was mostly directly related to the success which the men had in using the skill for which they had been trained, as is indicated by Table 8.5. Job mobility is greatest for the men in group B who, by definition, have to have held at least two jobs, one using their skill and one unskilled. However, men in this group seemed to have had a more disturbed time than others; 25 per cent of group B had more than 4 jobs compared with 11.7 per cent of the rest of the sample.

TABLE 8.5 *Job mobility compared with success in using training trade*

	A	*B*	*C*	*Total*
No jobs	—	—	1	1
			3.4	
One job	96	—	17	113
	54.2		*58.6*	
Two jobs	36	22	8	66
	20.3	*42.3*	*27.6*	
Three jobs	24	17	—	41
	13.6	*32.7*		
Four or more jobs	21	13	3	37
	11.9	*25.0*	*10.3*	
TOTAL	N = 177	52	29	258
	% = *100.0*	*100.0*	*99.9*	

Job mobility is also related to the age of the trainees, as Table 8.6 illustrates. The older men, 55.0 per cent of whom held only one job, were significantly less mobile than the 198 younger men; only 40.4 per cent of this latter group stayed in their first job, whilst only 2 of the 60 older men could be classified in the highly mobile group. It is understandable that the older men may be reluctant to job-hop. The length of unemployment which this group experienced prior to obtaining their first post-training job shows that finding employment was by and large not easy for them and one can imagine that having found a position they would not readily change jobs without careful consideration.

Difficulty in finding work after leaving the training centre seems to be directly related to lack of job mobility later. This is shown by the variations in job mobility according to area. Men from the Borders, the north-east and Fife where jobs were difficult to obtain all had less mobility than those from other areas. This may also be related to post-training 'success' of the trainees as the Borders and Fife both have low numbers of men who always used their skill and men from these areas also suffered longer initial un-employment. Like the older men, men from areas where employment is difficult may feel that once they have succeeded in getting a job they should hang on to it.

TABLE 8.6   *Relationship between job mobility and age*

	Under 40	Over 40	Total
No jobs	1 *0.5*	—	1
One job	80 *40.4*	33 *55.0*	113
Two jobs	47 *23.7*	19 *31.7*	66
Three jobs	35 *17.7*	6 *10.0*	41
Four or more jobs	35 *17.7*	2 *3.3*	37
TOTAL	N = 198 % = *100.0*	60 *100.0*	258

Training trade also affects mobility, as Table 8.7 indicates. This may be the result of different work patterns associated with different trades; for example among men working in the construction industry where employment tends to end with the completion of each contract held by the employer, a very high proportion held four or more jobs. This pattern of employment is not compatible with the arrangements made for construc-tion trainees under the 'improver' scheme mentioned earlier. In this scheme as was previously explained the trainees are expected to remain with their first employer during a probation period of sixty weeks.

TABLE 8.7   *Job mobility compared to training trade*

	One job	Four or more jobs	Total in each trade group
Construction	10 *16.9*	22 *37.3*	59
Engineering	55 *50.5*	9 *8.3*	109
Vehicle maintenance	11 *32.4*	4 *11.8*	34
Others	37 *66.1*	2 *3.6*	56
TOTAL	N = 113 % = *43.8*	37 *14.3*	258

Note: Percentages quoted are of the total numbers in each trade group.

During this period their earnings rise gradually from an initial 85 per cent of the craftsman's wage to the full rate. In practice, the construction trainees found that, once they had learnt some of the tricks of the trade, they could move to another site and, by keeping their background quiet, could quickly earn full skilled rates. A bit of judicious job-hopping was perceived as advantageous by these men. The simple fact is that if the trainee can get rid of the union card describing him as an 'improver' he is free to compete in the job market on equal terms with the time-served men. Low union density in the building industry was no doubt of help to these trainees.

Although the improver scheme may not be suited to the trades of the construction industry, it appeared to work successfully for the radio and television repairmen, as 13 of the 15 men studied held only one job. This may be the result of the apparent shortage of trained men in this trade which is discussed earlier (p. 94) rather than the result of the scheme itself.

Another measure of success is the earnings level attained by the men. One staggering discovery was the very low gross wages earned by the men in their first post-training job.[2] Table 8.8 shows that the trainees were the lowest paid of the adult work groups and made only a little more than the apprentices who had not finished their training when the first set of figures was obtained. The situation was improving by the end of the survey period. The rise in the wages of craftsmen and operators may be due to the inflation of the period of 1969–70, but the rises shown by apprentices and trainees also indicate the transition from inexperienced to experienced skilled men. This is particularly true in the case of the apprentices whose wage levels were catching up on the craftsmen's rates by the end of the eighteen months.

TABLE 8.8   *Average gross weekly earnings of trainees and control groups at the beginning and end of the survey period*

	Trainees £	Craftsmen £	Apprentices £	Operators £	Unemployed £
Finish/Interview date	18.8	25.1	17.9	20.2	—
18 months later	25.2	28.0	26.3	24.7	20.7

The trainees' wages become more meaningful when they are divided into different success groups as Table 8.9 indicates. Those who used their skill all the time are leading the field closely followed by those who never used their skill. Obviously those who could not use their training settled for a secure job with a reasonable earnings level. Their lack of mobility probably meant that they were climbing the earnings scale by seniority and somehow in their semi-skilled employment they managed to overtake the operators who were studied. It is the men in group B who earned least.

[2] If the wages given in the tables appear puny, it has to be remembered that just a few years of inflation play havoc with wage rates.

Their low initial wage may have contributed to their leaving their trades but it is surprising that they did not catch up with the other groups; perhaps the transfer between jobs of different skill levels meant that they did not gain experience in any one field during the eighteen months.

TABLE 8.9   *Average gross earnings for those who used their skill all the time (A), those who used their skill some of the time (B), and those who never used their skill (C)*

	A £	B £	C £
Finish date	20.0	17.0	18.9
18 months later	27.0	23.6	26.3
Number in group	177	52	29

Although the levels of earnings attained by the trainees compare favourably with men in other work groups they are poor compared to the levels which the trainees had expected to earn. During training they were asked to estimate the gross wage they expected to earn in their first post-training job and then in the job they would hold eighteen months after training ended. These guesses were compared with actual gross wages at the beginning of their first post-training employment and with actual gross wages earned when the final questionnaires were returned. Table 8.10 illustrates how far below anticipated earnings the actual wage levels lay. Initially, only one-quarter (25.3 per cent) of trainees had the sort of earnings they expected for their first jobs, and by the end of eighteen months less than one-fifth (17.2 per cent) had earnings which could be compared with their expectations. The numbers having greater than expected earnings is quite satisfactory until the high rate of inflation which occurred during 1969–70 is taken into consideration. The trainees were asked to complete the initial questionnaires in the autumn of 1968 and the spring of 1969 and it is unlikely that they amended their replies to take account of the rise in wages which was to come.

TABLE 8.10   *Success of trainees in meeting expectations of post-training earnings*

	First job after training %	*18 months after training* %
Greater than estimate	*32.3*	*45.9*
Equal to estimate	25.3	*17.2*
Less than estimate	39.3	*32.0*
Not known	3.1	*4.9*
TOTAL IN EMPLOYMENT	N = 257 % = *100.0*	244 *100.0*

It may now be useful to examine how the post-training situation fulfilled the hopes with which the trainees embarked on their courses. Fifty-eight of the trainees were disappointed right at the beginning of their training because they were unable to attend the courses they had chosen. The reasons which prevented their following the courses of their choice were health (10 men), long waiting lists for popular courses (17), failure to reach required standards of education (9), and other reasons governing availability of jobs in particular trades (22). One lesson to be learnt by the organisers of these courses is that every effort should be made to let men follow the trades they choose, as the 58 men who did not do this were significantly less successful than the others, as Table 8.11 shows.

TABLE 8.11   *Employment success of trainees who trained in the trade of their choice compared with success of those who were unable to attend the course of their choice*

	A	B	C	Total
Trained in trade of choice	146	36	18	200
	73.0	18.0	9.1	100.1
Did not train in trade of choice	31	16	11	58
	53.4	27.6	19.0	100.0
TOTAL	N = 177	52	29	258

This lack of success may be related to the fact that this group were much less satisfied with their training than the others. Eighteen months after they had left the government training centres only 65.5 per cent of these trainees were satisfied that they had attended government training centres compared with 82.0 per cent of the other men. This dissatisfaction may also stem from their inability to use their training, as level of satisfaction appears to be directly related to success in using training, as Table 8.12 illustrates. And we would refer back to our comments earlier (p. 24), when we argued the significance of a person's perception of the situation in which he finds

TABLE 8.12   *Level of satisfaction with attendance at government training centre compared with those who always used their skill (A), those who used their skill some of the time (B) and those who never used their skill (C)*

	A %	B %	C %	Total N
Very satisfied	55.4	15.4	13.8	110
Satisfied	36.7	36.5	27.6	92
Indifferent	5.1	21.2	34.5	30
Dissatisfied	2.8	25.0	24.1	25
Don't know	—	1.9	—	1
TOTAL	N = 177	52	29	258
	% = 100.0	100.0	100.0	

himself. Those who start a course of training feeling at least partly dissatisfied are likely to exhibit such emotions upon the completion of the course.

Another factor which influenced success in using the training skill was the pre-training situation of the man. Table 8.13 indicates that those trainees who were out of work when they applied for training were less successful in the post-training job market than the others; 28.9 per cent of the unemployed men never used their skill compared with 5.9 per cent of the previously employed men. Although the men who were unemployed prior to training had not managed to make as much use of their new skills as they presumably hoped, most were in some sort of employment at the end of the eighteen-month period. Only 7.5 per cent of those 106 men initially unemployed were still in the same circumstances at the end of the eighteen-month period, which compares well with 29.0 per cent of the 93 men in the unemployed control group who were still without work. There is no way of knowing whether or not the government training centre acted in the role of rehabilitation centre in helping these men return to work, or whether they could have made the transition successfully on their own initiative. It may be that men who have shown a measure of initiative are preferred by employers, even if the new skill is hardly utilised, and that the men themselves gain in morale by having recently been active.

TABLE 8.13   *Pre-training employment situation for those trainees who always used their skill (A), those who used their skill some of the time (B), and those who never used their skill (C)*

	A	B	C	Total
	%	%	%	N = 152
Employed	73.7	20.4	5.9	% = 100.0
				N = 106
Unemployed	51.3	19.8	28.9	% = 100.0

In order to assess how successful the training had been in meeting the trainees' ambitions the answers to the question of what motivated the men to seek training were re-examined. Realisation of the most popular motives – more security (205 men) and more satisfaction (203) – cannot be assessed from the data available. It is difficult to decide whether or not someone has achieved more job satisfaction and since this was not one of the research's objectives, no attempt was made to gauge job satisfaction as such. But as many of those who sought more satisfaction were among the more successful ones, there is a possibility that this search for a better job may have been realised. However, the third most popular reason, more money (197), if examined showed that not all those who wanted higher wages got them. However, 83 (42.1 per cent) of those men who wanted more money surpassed their previous earnings in their first post-training job, compared with 16 (26.2 per cent) of those 61 men who showed no apparent interest in training as a means to higher earnings. The reason for the difference between those who did not mention money and those who definitely did want more money is not just the result of one group being more money-conscious than the other. Those 61 men who did not mention money included 16 who mentioned only one reason for taking up training. For 8 of these men this reason was ill-health. In the total sample 15 men entered training for health reasons and 11 of them were understandably found in the non-money-minded group. This leads us to the tentative conclusion that where training is a forced issue, e.g. a decision precipitated by ill-health or unemployment, basic motivators are found, namely health reasons and security, and it is only when the decision to train is more voluntary that factors such as more job satisfaction and more money appear. This itself is supported by the finding that only 39 of the 61 men who did not mention money as a motivator mentioned satisfaction (63.9 per cent) compared with 82.8 per cent of the 197 men who wanted more money. Also the former group contained a higher percentage of those who were unemployed at the time of application (55.7 per cent) which compares with 36.5 per cent for the rest of the sample. Those who made no mention of money as a motivator did rather badly in getting suitable employment after training; only just over half of the 61 men were in group A compared with almost three-quarters of the 197 who sought money. It must be assumed that those 61 men who did not specially want more money as one of the rewards of training did rather worse than others in terms of earnings and job success, not just because they did not want more money but because they were underprivileged initially, handicapped by unemployment and ill-health.

GEOGRAPHICAL MOBILITY

In the period following training a certain amount of geographical mobility occurred. For some men this was a facet of their success, for others mobility was prompted by failure. Eighty-six trainees moved home during the study period, but the majority (51) of these moves were to a new house within the same town or to a town or village within easy access of the trainee's original community. The 35 remaining trainees who moved home made more radical changes to their way of life, moving too far to be able to have much contact with their previous environment and presumably making a new town the centre of their work and social life. It is only the men in this latter group who are considered as being 'geographically mobile'.

A higher percentage of trainees moved outside their local area (13.6 per cent) than men in the control groups who had a mobility rate of 10.1 per cent. The control group which had the greatest mobility was the apprentices (13.0 per cent), suggesting that the end of training produces a reaction against the restriction of apprenticeship life for some of these young men and a subsequent wish to savour freedom by moving around.[3] The timing

---

[3] But since the vast majority (87 per cent) of apprentices had not moved, it would be patently absurd to suggest that the end of an apprenticeship produces a mass exodus. Most stay put, it seems.

of the moves does suggest that mobility is particularly high immediately following the end of training. Twenty-two of the 35 mobile men moved within the first six months following training but only half that number moved in the following six months and only 8 trainees moved one year after training ended. (This total is more than 35 because some of the men made more than one move.) Perhaps the higher rates of geographical mobility exhibited by the trainees and apprentices will diminish within the first two years and reach rates similar to those of the craftsmen; here only a low 7.5 per cent of the 96 craftsmen moved home during the study period.

When asked why they had moved, 17 of the trainees stated they had done so in order to find suitable work. In this they were successful as all but one found jobs where they were able to use their training skills. Four men who moved to earn higher wages were also quite successful in finding 'skilled' jobs except for one man who was in skilled work until he returned to his home in Dundee where he took a job as a lorry driver. The remaining 14 mobile men moved due to domestic reasons. The men who moved for job or money reasons were more successful than those who moved for domestic reasons; 90.5 per cent of the former group always used their skill in comparison with 35.7 per cent of the latter.

The operators and unemployed groups who moved tended to do so for the same reason as the trainees, i.e. to seek better employment. In contrast, the craftsmen and apprentices who moved gave higher wages as their dominant reason. These last two groups would appear to be in the fortunate position of having the guarantee of a certain type of employment and their major preoccupation was, it seems, to sell their skill at the highest price.

The previous job history of the trainees who moved home showed that they tended to be men with several job and geographical changes prior to their training period. This was a tendency which could not be readily examined because of the different age distribution between the two groups of mobile and immobile; any examination which made comparisons of job history in terms of age would make cell sizes too small to be meaningful. However, of the 15 post-training mobile men who had made no geographical moves prior to training, 9 were aged under 25. The differences in the numbers of previously mobile men who moved after training and the previously immobile men who moved are only significant at the 10 per cent level for trainees but at the 5 per cent level for the three control groups (apprentices are omitted because of their limited job history), as Table 8.14 shows.

As a group the trainees had previously been much less mobile than any of the three adult control groups (operators, unemployed men and craftsmen). The lack of mobility of *some* of the trainees suggests that training was a means to avoid moving home *for them*. This was particularly true for men who had been miners in Fife. When many of these men were made redundant as a result of a pit fire they were offered alternative employment in mining in another area, and those miners who trained were in the main

TABLE 8.14   *Geographical mobility before and during study period*

Before After	Trainees		Controls [a]	
	Mobile	*Immobile*	*Mobile*	*Immobile*
Mobile	20	15	22	4
	18.0	*10.2*	*11.5*	*4.3*
Immobile	91	132	169	90
	82.0	*89.8*	*88.5*	*95.7*
TOTAL N =	111	147	191	94
% =	*100.0*	*100.0*	*100.0*	*100.0*

[a] Apprentices are omitted.

men who preferred to try for new employment in their own area rather than cling to a familiar job if it meant moving from their home area. One of the questions, asking the trainees what made them seek training, produced the response that 18.2 per cent of the trainees did so in order to avoid moving home. Whilst this was certainly not one of the major motivators (compare this with the 79.8 per cent who sought more security or the 79 per cent who wanted a more satisfying job – see Chapter 6, Table 6.8), it was a motivator for nearly one-fifth of the sample, of whom not a few were ex-miners.

From questions asked during training it appeared that those who proved to be mobile were much less attached to their home areas than the others, on the basis of their original statement. Some of the answers to these questions on mobility have to be treated with care as the trainees probably remembered that willingness to move was one of the criteria for acceptance on a training course. However, only 34.3 per cent of the 35 trainees who moved said that they preferred to find work in their home area compared with 83.4 per cent of the other 233 trainees.

Questions which investigated what the men had actually done about moving showed greater differences between the two groups than questions on what they thought they would do about moving. Perhaps this is another example of the interviewees giving those answers which they thought were expected rather than the true answers. Throughout this exercise we were made to realise time and again the value of longitudinal research, which highlighted the dangers of 'snapshot' questionnaires especially where these deal with anticipated behaviour; although one must not overstate the case. And past behaviour can be a guide. For example, two questions from the initial questionnaire illustrate the difference between mobility in theory and mobility in practice. One question asked, 'If you could not get a job locally in your training trade what would you do?'

1. Move to a job in your trade in another area?
2. Try to find a job in another trade in your home area?
3. Anything else? (give details)

Thirty-one of the mobile men (88.6 per cent) and 158 of the immobile trainees (70.8 per cent) said they would move. The second question asked, 'Have you in the last three years seriously considered moving to another area or abroad?' Of the migrant trainees 71.4 per cent had thought of moving compared with only 37.2 per cent of the non-migrant trainees. These findings suggest that if training is to be a device to aid manpower mobility then past activity rather than assurances of future mobility must be considered.

The same pattern repeats itself with the apprentices and craftsmen as Tables 8.15 and 8.16 indicate. In theory many men were quite willing to move although they had not given much consideration to the practicalities of moving. Even so, only 55.2 per cent of all craftsmen would move compared with 74.0 per cent of all trainees. It may be that the craftsmen in this sample who were all in regular employment using their trades when interviewed regarded the question of not finding a job in their trade as a rather unrealistic one, whereas for the trainees who had no direct experience of skilled jobs the possibility of not finding a job in their trade in their home area was a reality.

TABLE 8.15   '*If you could not get a job locally in your training trade what would you do?*'

	Trainees		Craftsmen		Apprentices	
	Mobile	*Immobile*	*Mobile*	*Immobile*	*Mobile*	*Immobile*
	%	*%*	*%*	*%*	*%*	*%*
Move to a job	*88.6*	*70.8*	*71.4*	*53.9*	*61.5*	*78.2*
Stay at home	*5.7*	*25.1*	*28.6*	*39.3*	*15.4*	*16.1*
Other	*5.7*	*3.1*	*—*	*5.6*	*15.4*	*2.3*
Don't know	*—*	*0.9*	*—*	*1.1*	*7.7*	*3.5*
TOTAL N =	35	223	7	89	13	87
% =	*100.0*	*99.9*	*100.0*	*99.9*	*100.0*	*100.1*

TABLE 8.16   '*Have you in the last three years seriously considered moving to another area or abroad?*'

	Trainees		Craftsmen		Apprentices	
	Mobile	*Immobile*	*Mobile*	*Immobile*	*Mobile*	*Immobile*
	%	*%*	*%*	*%*	*%*	*%*
No	*25.7*	*62.8*	*42.9*	*71.9*	*38.5*	*71.3*
Yes	*71.4*	*37.2*	*57.1*	*28.1*	*61.6*	*28.7*
Immigrant	*2.9*	*—*	*—*	*—*	*—*	*—*
TOTAL N =	35	223	7	89	13	87
% =	*100.0*	*100.0*	*100.0*	*100.0*	*100.1*	*100.0*

One point which clearly distinguished the mobile from the immobile trainees was that many of the former had lived in digs during their training period. Of the 35 mobile trainees 82.9 per cent were in digs compared with 54 (24.2 per cent) of immobile trainees. This suggests that someone who is prepared to live away from home for six or twelve months to attend a training course has no home ties strong enough to bind him to one area, or alternatively, having lived away from home for a fairly long period, the trainee is prepared to repeat the experience. The other relevant factor may be that those men who were living in digs came from areas outside the Scottish central industrial belt and these areas tend to have limited employment opportunities. For many people from these areas there is a tradition that it is necessary to move to central Scotland or to England in order to get a 'decent' job. This tradition of moving in order to obtain a decent job is likely to be found in certain other parts of the UK. For us this tradition was exemplified by the disproportionate number of mobile trainees who came from the north-east and Angus (see Table 8.17).

TABLE 8.17   *Original location of mobile and immobile trainees*

	Mobile	*Immobile*
The Lothians	7	88
	20.0	*39.5*
Fife	7	67
	20.0	*30.0*
Angus	5	11
	14.3	*4.9*
North-east	7	24
	20.0	*10.8*
Borders	1	5
	2.9	*2.2*
Industrial west	5	12
	14.3	*5.4*
Others	3	16
	8.6	*7.2*
TOTAL N =	35	223
% =	*100.1*	*100.0*

Most of the mobile men were aged under 25, as Table 8.18 shows. Mobility then tailed off until the 36–40 age group when a significantly higher number of men in the control groups moved and there was also a slightly increased tendency for trainees of this age to move. It is not easy to find an explanation for this burst of activity in the 36–40 age group. There are no obvious differences in the ages of their children or the size of their families as compared to other age groups which might explain these moves. Perhaps one explanation of the mobility can be found in the concept of the 'mid-life crisis' which has been discussed by Rapoport[4] among others. Mid-life is seen as a period when the physical and mental powers

[4] R. N. Rapoport, *Mid-Career Development* (Tavistock, 1970), pp. 136–8.

of man begin to decline and the man is brought to the point where he will stand back and start questioning his values and commitments in the light of this self-knowledge. There are numerous ways in which a man may resolve this crisis, one of which may be to seek a new job (the trainees do this) in a new environment.

TABLE 8.18   *Age of mobile and immobile groups*

	Trainees		Controls	
	Mobile	*Immobile*	*Mobile*	*Immobile*
	%	%	%	%
25 and under	*48.6*	*28.7*	*26.9*	*17.0*
26–30	*20.0*	*22.9*	*19.2*	*21.2*
31–35	*11.4*	*15.2*	*19.2*	*16.6*
36–40	*8.6*	*8.1*	*26.9*	*12.7*
41 and over	*11.4*	*25.1*	*7.7*	*32.4*
TOTAL N =	35	223	26	259
% =	*100.0*	*100.0*	*99.9*	*99.9*

No marked differences were observed in the mobility of the married and unmarried men. Among the control groups it did seem that the most mobile men were those who experienced a change in marital status during the study period, i.e. the five who married and one who got a divorce, but no significance can be attached to this difference.

One factor which did appear to make a difference to the mobility of these men was the type of housing in which they lived. Rossi [5] has shown that in the USA those who own property are not willing to move and it is people who rent housing who are mobile. Very few of the trainees in Scotland owned their homes and those who did were divided proportionately between the mobile and immobile: 11.4 per cent of the mobile men owned their homes and 11.7 per cent of the immobile trainees did so.

The housing situation in Scotland is unique in that a very high proportion of the population has local authority housing; 53.3 per cent of housing is rented from the local authority and 14.4 per cent from private landlords, compared with 28.1 per cent and 17.8 per cent respectively for the rest of Great Britain.[5] It may be that renting council property in Scotland takes on the same significance as owning a house does in the USA. Once a family has succeeded in working themselves up the waiting list to get a house they become reluctant to leave in case they should find themselves at the end of another housing list in some other town. The difference in mobility between those who rented council property and others was significant at the 5 per cent level: only 37.1 per cent of the 35 mobile trainees rented council housing initially as compared with 58.3 per cent of the 223 men who did not move home.

[5] P. H. Rossi, *Why Families Move* (Free Press of Glencoe, 1955).
[6] Housing and Construction Statistics No. 9, First Quarter 1974, p. 73.

CONCLUSION

Information from the post-training experiences of the 258 men studied showed the training to be relatively successful; all but 11.2 per cent had a chance to use their skill at some time, and 68.6 per cent seemed to have settled in employment in their trades. Some factors contributing to success have been identified: men who entered training from regular employment were more successful than those who were unemployed prior to their government training centre course; also if men did not get jobs within a short time of completing their training the chances of getting a job in their trade fell as unemployment lengthened, and certain trades appear to have a higher rate of employment success than others. Trainees made an initial financial loss which showed in lower income levels during and after training compared to pre-training earnings, but this loss appeared to be compensated for by higher earnings at the end of the study period. Although willingness to move is judged to be necessary for a trainee's post-training geographical mobility, such mobility had in fact little effect on levels of success in using training skills. Geographical mobility appears to be related only to age, previous geographical mobility and housing, and not to training or employment factors.

Chapter 9

Industrial Relations Aspects
of Skills Dilution[1]

INTRODUCTION

The craft apprenticeship tradition and the long history of resistance to any form of 'skills dilution' must be considered in any assessment of the government training effort, for one of the most pressing problems for the ex-trainees was to gain acceptance from all pertinent sectors of the working population – time-served craftsmen, employers, and trade unions (especially their shop-floor representatives). All three will be discussed below, but first of all concern is given to the men with whom the trainees came into contact most – the craftsmen, apprentices and shop stewards. The first two groups formed control groups for the research project, but when it became apparent from the first postal questionnaires that a significant proportion of trainees were meeting some difficulties in becoming accepted by the skilled labour force, 62 shop stewards and 38 employers in Scotland were interviewed in order to assess their attitude to government training.

To gauge the magnitude of resistance to (and acceptance of) 'skills dilution' the same two questions were put to members of the three groups. They were first asked their views on the retraining of craftsmen whose apprenticeship skill was now redundant and secondly on the training of men who had never obtained an apprenticeship skill; the answers to these questions are given in Tables 9.1 and 9.2. It will be observed that the final-year apprentices were the least 'liberal' of the work-groups. Financial arguments formed the main basis for their judgement not to allow people who had not undergone an apprenticeship to be trained; their view frequently was not that people had 'missed' the chance but that they had not wished to serve an apprenticeship and had 'gone for the big money' in a hedonistic way, i.e. taken jobs which offered no training but paid well while their peers were earning very little as apprentices. The support which these opinions get is shown in Table 9.3.

---

[1] Some preliminary material of this chapter has been published in a different format elsewhere, see *British Journal of Industrial Relations* (March 1970).

TABLE 9.1 · *Attitude of shop stewards, craftsmen and apprentices to trade training for redundant craftsmen*

Question		Shop Stewards	Craftsmen	Apprentices
Do you think that	Yes	58	88	91
there should be		*93.5*	*91.7*	*91.0*
facilities for	Doubtful	2	2	6
retraining people		*3.3*	*2.1*	*6.0*
whose apprenticeship	No	2	4	3
trade has become		*3.3*	*4.2*	*3.0*
redundant?	Don't know	—	2	—
			2.1	
	TOTAL N =	62	96	100
	% =	*100.1*	*100.1*	*100.0*

Note: Throughout the chapter figures in italics in the tables indicate percentages.

TABLE 9.2   *Attitude of shop stewards, craftsmen and apprentices to trade training for men who never served an apprenticeship*

Question		Shop Stewards	Craftsmen	Apprentices
Do you think that	Yes	44	65	41
there should be		*71.0*	*67.7*	*41.0*
facilities for	Doubtful	13	9	14
retraining people		*21.0*	*9.4*	*14.0*
who missed the	No	5	21	45
chance of an		*8.0*	*21.9*	*45.0*
apprenticeship?	Don't know	—	1	—
			1.0	
	TOTAL N =	62	96	100
	% =	*100.0*	*100.0*	*100.0*

DILUTEE ACCEPTANCE AND PAST APPRENTICESHIPS

The first point to be noted from the tables is that in virtually every case responses indicated that acceptance of trainees rather than outright rejection was the more prominent attitude exhibited. Indeed, to many who expect the stereotype of outright rejection of dilution, the figures obtained may come as a surprise. Yet there are indications that a not insignificant porportion of 'traditional' craftsmen could be expected to resist dilution by at least some of the ex-trainees and if this is so then it is worthwhile to analyse the effect of such resistance.

Whilst the reasons shown in Table 9.3 might hold good for some trainees, they are by no means true for all. Firstly not all the trainees had the chance of an apprenticeship. Exactly one-third of the men certainly had the opportunity but did not make the best use of it; this covers the 86 men who started apprenticeship training but did not complete it. And there were 22 men who had completed apprenticeships. The majority of the sample, however – 150 men or 58.1 per cent – had not even started training. The most frequent reason for failing to begin indentured training was 'could not get one', quoted by 52 men (34.7 per cent of those who did not commence an apprenticeship), followed by frank 'not interested' from 33 trainees (22.0 per cent) with the remaining 65 men (43.3 per cent) producing a variety of reasons ranging from financial and domestic problems to ignorance of craft training.

TABLE 9.3   *Reason for not allowing men who missed the chance of an apprenticeship to be trained*

	Shop Stewards	*Craftsmen*	*Apprentices*
Training not adequate	—	4	3
Went for the 'big money'	—	3	12
Had their chance before	1	7	10
Various others a	4	7	20
TOTAL	N = 5	21	45

a This category encompassed a whole host of reasons too numerous to include and each quoted by the odd person or two, such as 'well I served my time', 'once you start this, where will it end?', 'we don't want them', 'it will reduce our security', 'it will reduce our bargaining strength', etc.

THE 'FREE' SKILLED TICKET MYTH

It has to be admitted that the trainees, upon leaving school, had in fact gone after 'big money' – a 14- or 15-year-old boy was almost bound to get more money in most jobs than his apprentice friends. The trainees, however, pay for getting a skill in later life, and this sacrifice may be compared with that which the apprentice has made in his teens. Thus while their apprentice friends, now qualified craftsmen, were earning the skilled rates, the trainees took a drop from their previous earning rate during and following their training period, as is shown in Table 9.4.

It will be observed that training allowances represented a drop in income for over three-quarters of the Scottish trainees, i.e. 77.9 per cent. The actual drop is rather difficult to measure as the allowances are tax-free which makes them more valuable for most men, but a lodging allowance is often included so that the money left to the man was frequently not as much as at first appears. The lodging allowances in fact explain the circumstances of quite a number of the 16 Scots who seemed to get more than they had previously earned – 10 of these men were living in digs (62.5 per cent of 16 compared with 27.9 per cent living in lodgings for the total Scottish sample).

In addition to the training period when they had a low level of income, the trainees did not immediately rise to a level equivalent to their previous earnings, for in order to take account of the inflation which occurred

TABLE 9.4   *Comparison of training allowance and first post-training earnings with pre-training earnings of trainees*

| | Scotland | | Liverpool | |
	Allowance	First job	Allowance	First job
Greater than pre-	16	99	1	11
training earnings	*6.2*	*38.4*	*3.0*	*33.3*
Equal to pre-	41	60	4	8
training earnings	*15.9*	*23.3*	*12.1*	*24.2*
Less than pre-	201	92	28	12
training earnings	*77.9*	*35.7*	*84.8*	*36.4*
Don't know	—	7	—	2
		2.7		*6.1*
TOTAL N =	258	258	33	33
% =	*100.0*	*100.1*	*99.9*	*100.1*

during their six or twelve months' courses the trainees would have had to exceed their previous earnings level in order to maintain their pre-training standard of living. However, at the end of the eighteen-month period most had started to compensate for these losses in income, had overtaken the earnings of the operators, and were rapidly catching up with the craftsmen, as Table 9.5 indicates. It would therefore appear that a government training course does not give one a free 'skilled ticket' – as with more traditional craftsmen, it has to be 'bought' via forgone earnings.

TABLE 9.5   *Average earnings for all groups at the beginning and end of the survey period*

	Scotland £	Liverpool £	Craftsmen £	Apprentices £	Operators £	Unemployed £
Initial wage	18.8	20.0	25.1	17.9	20.2	—
Wage at 18 months	25.2	29.4	28.0	26.3	24.7	20.7

THE SHOP STEWARDS' ATTITUDES

Readers of certain sectors of the popular press may be forgiven for assuming that shop stewards as a genre are bloody-minded and illiberal, and if this is so then it would be logical to assume that shop stewards representing skilled men would not be 'liberal' in their attitudes towards trainees. Yet Table 9.2 shows that they are in fact even more liberal than many of their constituents – perhaps only a small point, but one worth bearing in mind when listening to sweeping generalisations as regards this body of men. In each of the three groups there are roughly similar proportions of men who agree to retraining for craftsmen whose skills are redundant (Table 9.1); and most shop stewards (71.0 per cent) and craftsmen (67.7 per cent) would allow men 'who missed the chance of an apprenticeship' to be retrained but less than half (41.0 per cent) of the apprentices would agree to this training (see Table 9.2). These differences between stewards and apprentices and craftsmen and apprentices are statistically significant at the 0.1 per cent level.

Given that the majority of shop stewards may be aware of the traditional aspects of orthodox apprenticeships, and certainly ought to be conversant with the control function of this method of skills acquisition, it was thought that an exercise comprising a visit to a government training centre by a group of shop stewards might be of interest in so far as one might then assess the opinions exhibited towards this method of skills training prior to and after the visit. This was part of a larger exercise in which 38 firms were visited in order to obtain management and shop-floor trade union attitudes to government training, as has already been suggested on the first page of this chapter. Some of the stewards had already come into contact with trainees as twenty-five of the thirty-eight firms in which they worked employed, or had at some time employed, trainees. These firms had been chosen to match the geographical and industrial spread of the Scottish trainee sample as far as was practicably possible. Although some stewards had indirect contact with government training centres in their employing organisations, it was decided to arrange for a small group of stewards to visit a government training centre so that they could see how the courses were run and the facilities available for training. The smallness of this sample of shop stewards was disappointing and was in the main due to the unwillingness of some employers to release their men for the best part of one day. An attempt was made to gauge any change in attitudes due to this visit by asking the stewards to complete a short questionnarire after the visit and then to discuss their impressions of the training and of the training centres; three months later, further questionnaires were sent to this group in order to ascertain if there had been any change in the attitudes

TABLE 9.6   *Comparison of attitudes towards government training centres held by shop stewards who visited a training centre with those of other shop stewards*

Do you feel that the Government's scheme for training adults in craft skills is:	Stewards visiting GTC			Other stewards	
	First question-naire	*After visit*	*3 months later*	*First question-naire*	*3 months after GTC visit by other stewards*
Very poor	—	—	—	—	—
Poor	2	—	—	2	1
Adequate	1	—	1	3	1
Good	3	6	4	2	1
Very good	—	2	3	—	—
Don't know	2	—	—	1	5

exhibited immediately after the visit. At the same time a similar question-naire was sent to a matched group of stewards (in the same age range and the same trade unions) who had not visited the centre, in order to act as controls for this small experiment.

The numbers involved in this exercise were far too small to provide any-thing other than a very tentative conclusion. Table 9.6 does suggest that the stewards who were able to judge the standards of government training for themselves held more favourable attitudes than did those men who relied upon hearsay and contact with only one or two trainees. So at least in terms of quality of training government training centres would appear to have little to fear.

THE EMPLOYERS

As well as studying the attitudes which work people hold towards trainees the attitudes of the employers were also examined. Employers here usually meant personnel managers or persons responsible for hiring and firing manual workers. Thirty-eight employers were interviewed and the majority of these (25 or 65.8 per cent) had employed trainees at some time; 17 or 68.0 per cent of this group of 25 companies had hired them to meet short-ages of skilled labour. Eleven companies had hired the trainees to do semi-skilled work which, in five cases, led to skilled work; the other companies had placed trainees in skilled work immediately. Of the 13 employers who had not hired trainees, 5 said that they had a sufficiently large pool of time-served craftsmen to fill their requirements. The others did have shortages of skilled men but did not use government trained men in the main because of doubts that these men would manage to achieve the standard of work required.

Only 15 of the 38 companies had agreements with their unions about hiring trainees; naturally companies employing trainees had agreements more often than others, but 9 out of the 13 organisations who had not employed trainees had no agreement and 8 had not even attempted to dis-cuss the subject with their union representatives. Seven of these last 8 companies felt at the time of the interview that they had problems with shortages of skilled labour and, although part of the reluctance to hire trainees stemmed from doubts about their work standards as mentioned above, 4 claimed that 'the unions would not admit government training centre men'. It became clear that these employers, fearing an explosive situation, had never raised the topic of dilutee labour with their unions and were basing their replies on how they thought the representatives would act. This problem of lack of communication was evident during the visits to these companies; the interviewer first met the employer, then the stewards and discussed similar questions with each group – one group did not know the response of the other, and contradictory answers were often obtained. For example, in one company the employer stated that he could not employ trainees because the stewards would oppose this action; the stewards, however, said that they had never been approached on the subject and that they would give any trainee a fair chance of employment. The reverse of this situation occurred in another plant where the stewards declared their willingness to have trainees employed in the plant, but claimed that the production manager would not allow them. The manager, however, said later that his only criteria for employment were ability and willingness and that he did not care how the employee had gained his knowledge. It would therefore appear that communication between the two sides of industry is certainly one problem and if this is so then there is a need for improvement here, if a solution is to be found to some of the difficulties of employing trainees. What one may conclude at this point is that resistance to dilution is to some extent present within all sectors of the affected parts of the industrial community, but that its magnitude has been grossly exaggerated.

THE POSITION OF TRADE UNION OFFICIALS

To ascertain how deeply trade union officials are involved in the problems of the employment of government training centre trainees, regional officers of trade unions expected to recruit trainees were interviewed. Table 9.7 gives some details of the information obtained during the interviews.

The details given in Table 9.7 explain the national agreements reached between employers, unions and government training centres but do not explain the situation at branch or district level where a lot of decisions were apparently made. The local union officials appeared to know how far the national agreements are adhered to, but none seemed to take an active part in branch arrangements. In the same way, these officials kept out of any involvement with government training centres. The Department of Employment is keen for union representatives to sit on the selection panels which interview prospective entrants to their trade; this is usual in many parts of England, but only one of the Scottish officials interviewed attended these sessions with any regularity. Two had attended occasionally and the other two had never attended.

None of the discussions with the craftsmen, shop stewards or union officials suggested any strong antagonism to the trainees. Contact with the apprentices did suggest some antagonism but these men are too young to have much power in the workplace. It is, however, obviously important to see how the trainees viewed their reception in the work environment, for the trainees' subjective assessment of their acceptance by the people with whom they work can be critical in helping or hindering a trainee to settle.[2] At best, the awareness of ready acceptance must aid his establishment in the work force; at worst, the feeling of general antagonism may make a

---

[2] This was discussed in the Introduction under the 'Action Frame of Reference'. Its significance can hardly be exaggerated, for obviously in the final analysis it is the subjective judgement by the trainee of his actual or anticipated reception which may be crucial to his full integration in the pertinent labour market.

TABLE 9.7 *Regulations of five trade unions concerning membership for men trained in government training centres*

	Grade of membership	Dilution agreement	Rate of pay	Level of decision for accepting trainees
AUEW	Grade E	Yes	Rate for the job [b]	District
ASW	Trainee to full member in 60 weeks	No	Percentage rate [c]	National
AUBTW	Trainee to full member in 60 weeks	No	Percentage rate [c]	Branch
'Boilermakers'	None [a]	No	Not applicable	Branch
EETU/ PTU	Full member	No	Rate for the job [b]	National

[a] This union includes ex-trainees with other adult entrants to its trade and asks that these men serve five years with one company before achieving craft status. The six months' training scheme does not count towards this training.

[b] Motor mechanics come under the same scheme as members of the ASW (Amalgamated Society of Woodworkers) and AUBTW (Amalgamated Union of Building Trades Workers) (see note [c]).

[c] The trainee earns a percentage of the full craftsman's rate, varying from 85 per cent to 100 per cent after sixty weeks. During the sixty weeks 'improver' period the Department of Employment makes a small grant to the employer.

trainee decide to leave his training trade. To discover what sort of reception the trainees had received, they were asked in relation to each job held during the course of the research period how they had been received by trade unions (which in general meant its shop-floor representatives), by employers and by work-mates. This information was obtained for each job held by the trainees.

SKILLS UTILISATION

The reception the trainees received from unions, employers, and work-mates should be relevant only for those who were using their new skill at work; the acceptance of someone in a job where he was not using his training skill should be no different from that accorded to any other unskilled worker as, apart from possible personality problems, there should be no source of antagonism. On the other hand, someone who is using his skill and is perhaps labelled as a 'dilutee', either officially or unofficially, may give rise to these feelings which some craftsmen and apprentices expressed above (see Table 9.3). In actual fact, there are no significant differences between the men who used their skill and the others, as Table 9.8 indicates. Details are given for those using their skill and those not using their skill in each of their first three jobs and column 4 gives a total

TABLE 9.8   *Comparison of acceptance by trade unions of men using their training skill and those in jobs making no use of their training (Scottish trainees only)*

	Job 1		Job 2		Job 3		4 or more jobs	
	Using	Not using	Using	Not using	Using	Not using	Using	Not using
Very good	75	8	43	16	24	6	22	2
	62.5	61.5	69.4	84.2	72.7	66.7	66.7	100.0
Good	39	3	16	3	9	3	11	—
	32.5	23.1	25.8	15.8	27.3	33.3	33.3	
Poor	5	1	3	—	—	—	—	—
	4.2	7.7	4.8					
Not at all	1	1	—	—	—	—	—	—
	0.8	7.7						
TOTAL N =	120	13	62	19	33	9	33	2
% =	100.0	100.0	100.0	100.0	100.0	100.0	100.0	100.0
Don't know	6	1	11	3	2	2	6	—
No union member-ship	94	23	48	21	23	10	18	12
	42.7	62.2	29.7	48.8	39.7	47.6	31.6	85.7
TOTAL N =	220	37	121	43	58	21	57	14

for those with four or more jobs in order to give figures large enough for analysis. Comparisons have been made only for those who were members of unions and who provided information on their acceptance by unions. As can be seen, there are no differences in the proportions of those using their skill and those in 'unskilled' jobs who state that their acceptance was 'very good', so one must assume that the majority of trainees had as good a relationship with their union as any other working group. The only interesting difference is that more of the trainees working in their training trade are union members than the others. This tendency increased with the number of jobs held until more than two-thirds of the job-hoppers who had four or more jobs were union members (see Table 9.8). This suggests that membership of the appropriate union may be a prerequisite for job mobility.

The hypothesis that the perception of poor treatment by the trainees may be instrumental in making them leave their training trade is supported by the different perceived acceptance accorded to trainees who used their trade in all jobs and those who used their trade only sometimes. Table 9.9 indicates the numbers who thought their union reception had been 'very good' among members of the A group and the B group who were using their skill in Job 1, 2 or 3[3] and gives the difference between the two groups as statistically significant at the 0.1 per cent level. It must be pointed out that many of these assessments cannot be described as trainees making accusations against the unions once they had failed; the assessments were taken from the small intermediary questionnaires which were often completed *during* the job tenure and not retrospectively.[4] The figures involved in the Liverpool sample are too small to give any clear evidence for the hypothesis that poor reception of a trainee by his union can be a factor contributing to his abandonment of his training trade and are therefore excluded – yet in so far as they can be assessed they do not contradict the foregoing.

Any differences in reception for those who only used their skill temporarily in Jobs 2 and 3 are not so obvious since the numbers are rather small. What can be pointed out is how union membership drops for those who had not managed to be permanently settled in employment in their training

TABLE 9.9   *Union acceptance of the trainees who used their skill all the time (A) and those who used their skills only for a short time (B) when in skills-related jobs*

		Job 1		Job 2		Job 3	
		A	B	A	B	A	B
Very good		69	6	37	6	22	2
		69.0	*30.0*	*72.5*	*54.5*	*75.9*	*50.0*
Good		27	12	12	4	7	2
		27.0	*60.0*	*23.5*	*36.4*	*24.1*	*50.0*
Poor		4	1	2	1	—	—
		4.0	*5.0*	*3.9*	*9.1*		
Not at all		—	1	—	—	—	—
			5.0				
TOTAL	N =	100	20	51	11	29	4
	% =	*100.0*	*100.0*	*99.9*	*100.0*	*100.0*	*100.0*
Don't know		5	2	7	4	2	—
No union member-		73	20	24	24	15	8
ship		*41.0*	*47.6*	*29.3*	*61.5*	*32.6*	*66.6*
TOTAL	N =	178	42	82	39	46	12

trade. Thus in Job 2 only 38.5 per cent of the 39 B trainees were union members compared with 70.7 per cent of the A group, and in Job 3 only

[3] Beyond Job 3 numbers become too small to be meaningful.

[4] Indeed, one of the most cogent arguments in favour of longitudinal studies is that experiences and attitudes are monitored as they take place and not *post hoc*, with all that that implies in terms of faulty memory and rationalisation.

one-third of the B group were members although some two-thirds of the others held union membership. For Job 2 the difference in union membership for the two groups is statistically significant at the 0.1 per cent level. It is of course not possible to know whether the men were not union members from choice or through necessity, but for many it is probably the latter case as only 7 out of the 258 men had stated that they would not be prepared to join a trade union when they filled in the initial questionnaire.

PERCEPTION OF TRADE UNION ATTIDUDES

The trainees' feelings regarding their acceptance by the various trade unions were compared for each of the five craft unions mentioned in Table 9.7. as they existed prior to union mergers during the research period. From that table it would have appeared that antagonism towards the trainees would be most likely in the Boilermakers' Union [5] who do not recognise trainees, and in the engineering union (the AUEW) with their policy of labelling trainees as 'dilutees'. Antagonism ought to have been least likely from the ASW and AUBTW (the two building trade unions) which have clearly defined routes for trainees to gain acceptance as skilled men, and from the electrical trade union (the EETU/PTU) which has no embargo upon trainees. Yet Table 9.10 would seem to indicate [6] that, apart from the electrical trade union who fulfil these expectations, the reverse of the expected situation occurs. Although the Boilermakers' Society has a policy not to accept trainees into membership, one trainee did succeed in obtaining membership and he claimed to have been very well received; this man admitted, however, that he obtained his membership by not 'letting on' where he learned his trade, in which case his treatment will logically be that accorded to time-served men. Later one other man managed to obtain membership of this union and one must presume that he used similar tactics in order to obtain entry. A welder from Liverpool was not so smart and wrote about the difficulties he had in getting work without having a Boilermakers' card, although he was a member of the AUEW; his final comment summed up his problem as he saw it – 'the bloody unions run this country'. The four members of the AUBTW were contented with being members of that union, but the 35 men who joined the ASW were not all enthusiastic about the reception which they received; a hint of the difficulties trainees in this union had was a comment from a joiner in Fife who stated that the 'local trade union was unwilling to accept trainees (on no a vote of members) but directive from their head office forced them to accept us'. The men who joined the AUEW appeared in the main pleased by the way in which they were treated.

[5] The Amalgamated Society of Boilermakers, Shipwrights, Blacksmiths and Structural Workers.

[6] Any conclusions drawn from Table 9.10 can only be tentative due to the small numbers involved.

TABLE 9.10   *Acceptance from each union for those Scottish trainees who*
were union members and used their skill in the first job

	AUEW %	ASW %	AUBTW %	EETU/ PTU %	Boilermakers %
Very good	72.2	50.0	75.0	77.8	100.0
Good	20.4	47.1	25.0	22.2	—
Poor	5.6	2.9	—	—	—
Not at all	1.9	—	—	—	—
TOTAL N =	54	34	4	9	1
% =	100.1	100.0	100.0	100.0	100.0
Don't know N =	3	1	—	1	—

The above analysis suggests that clearly defined rules and regulations governing the acceptance of trainees into membership of a trade union are no guarantee of producing a situation where the trainee feels that he is accepted. This is an example of the wide breach which can exist between union officialdom and membership: official rules may then not be adhered to because they are not the kind of rules that the union members want. An obvious example of this is when local memberships have sometimes shown their power in strikes which have been in opposition to their national organisation. And this might suggest that rank and file local members not infrequently contradict national rulings on the acceptance of trainees. It would therefore appear that not only have the government training centre officials to reach agreement with union leaders but that they must also woo the rank and file to win their acceptance of men trained in government training centres. Many of the trainees who felt that they were not treated as well as they might have been were in fact those who left their training trade after one job or after a short time in a 'skilled' job (see Table 9.9).

Despite these problems, the comments which the trainees wrote on their questionnaires to enlarge upon some of the answers they had given in filling in the forms, concentrated not on difficulties of union membership but on difficulties with employers and work-mates, as Table 9.11 indicates. As these comments were entirely spontaneous, it is not possible to draw very many conclusions from them since they come mainly from the more literate members of the sample. It is obvious, however, that the men must have felt very strongly about these matters to sit down and write, often in great detail, about the difficulties which they had faced. One point to be noted is that the frequency of these comments diminished over the eighteen-month period; either trainees had come to terms with these problems and had managed to surmount them in some way, or else they had given up their training trade and so no longer encountered these difficulties.

TABLE 9.11   *Comments from trainees on their reception at work*

	Scotland			Liverpool		
	6 months	12 months	18 months	6 months	12 months	18 months
Get GTC to negotiate with unions for recognition for trainees	4	1	2	—	—	—
No chance of union membership	4	1	—	1	1	—
Resistance from stewards	2	1	—	—	—	—
Resistance from employers	24	13	8	2	1	1
Resistance from work-mates	9	2	1	1	—	—
General resistance	11	5	—	5	2	1
No comments	159	162	247	21	21	31
TOTAL	213	185	258	30	25	33
No reply to this questionnaire	45	73	—	3	8	—

DIFFICULTIES WITH EMPLOYERS

The comments which trainees made on difficulties from employers can be divided into two main categories. The first of these dealt with the difficulty of finding an employer who was prepared to hire a trainee; this was mentioned by 26 of the 45 men making remarks about employers. Typical comments here were 'no prospective employer would look at you when they discovered you came from a government training centre (hairdresser from Fife) or 'employers don't want to know' (motor mechanic from West Lothian).[7] Many of the pertinent group of men were discouraged by the number of interviews which they had attended without success; 5 of the 26 mentioned with surprise the number of well-known firms who treated their job applications discourteously. One of the organisations which excelled in barring trainees was a government establishment and one trainee was very puzzled that he should have been helped by the government to do his training course only to be refused admittance to a government workshop. Two other trainees suggested that the courses would only be successful if employers were 'made to co-operate in these schemes and employ these men'.

The second problem with employers was mentioned by 16 of the trainees and dealt with 'exploitation' once they had found an employer to hire

---

[7] Similar comments were received from the Liverpool trainees.

them. 'It's cheap labour they're after,' was a frequent comment here. Thus one motor mechanic stated that 'many bosses want you to work for considerably less money than a craftsman' and a typewriter mechanic said that he would have to wait two years before getting full pay. To substantiate the thesis of exploitation is difficult; it has to be accepted that many trainees, after an accelerated course, may not be able to perform their skill speedily enough to earn a bonus, and trainees are not unique in being disappointed with lower wages than those suggested during recruitment. But the claim of exploitation cannot easily be brushed aside.

These feelings of being treated rather badly by employers are borne out when the trainees' assessment of their acceptance by employers is studied. Table 9.12 shows acceptance by trade unions, employers and employees for both Scottish and Liverpool trainees using their training in their first job. Although slightly more of both groups of trainees reckon they were

TABLE 9.12   *Acceptance by trade unions, employers and employees in the first job for men using their skill*

	Scotland			Liverpool		
	Trade unions	Employers	Employees	Trade unions	Employers	Employees
Very good	75	120	123	9	12	17
	62.5	*5.4*	*58.9*	*42.9*	*37.5*	*53.1*
Good	39	68	65	9	16	14
	32.5	*32.5*	*31.1*	*42.9*	*50.0*	*43.8*
Poor	5	21	18	3	4	1
	4.2	*10.0*	*9.0*	*14.3*	*12.5*	*3.1*
Not at all	1	—	3	—	—	—
	0.8		*1.4*			
TOTAL N =	120	209	209	21	32	32
% =	*100.0*	*99.9*	*100.0*	*100.1*	*100.0*	*100.0*
Don't know	6	10	10	3	—	—
N/a [a]	94	1	1	8	—	—
TOTAL N =	220	220	220	32	—	—

[a] Not applicable – this includes men who were not union members and also one man who was self-employed.

treated 'very well' by unions than thought they were so treated by employers, these differences are not statistically significant. However, there are significant differences for Scottish trainees when one considers the number saying that their treatment from employers and from trade unions was 'poor'; this is significant at the 5 per cent level.

For the Scottish trainees, a pattern similar to that for unions appears for the reported treatment from employees, although the number of comments received on this topic (12) was not as high as the number of complaints regarding unions (15) – see Table 9.11. The comments referring to work-mates included 'little animosity from time-served men' (instrument mechanic, Edinburgh) and 'touch of hostility' (welder, West Lothian). The Liverpool trainees rated treatment from work-mates as better than that from unions or employers.

The amount of resistance credited to the employers and work-mates must be partly due to the fact that these are the people with whom the trainees had direct contact rather than the union officials, which is what the term 'trade union' must have meant to some trainees at least. Yet for the majority the term 'trade union' meant the union's shop-floor representative, as is indicated for instance by a centre-lathe turner from Fife who wrote 'employers are often willing to take a trainee but the unions won't let them', or the agricultural fitter who stated that 'union opposition prevented my obtaining the job I wanted', when in each of these cases it could hardly have been the union at national level or its district organiser off his own bat to whom responsibility could be assigned.

Although some of the difficulties can be put against either employers, employees or unions, many problems arise from a general feeling of hostility which can run through a place of work yet cannot definitely be blamed on any one specific group.

As a final exercise on this topic it was decided to examine the trainees'

TABLE 9.13   *Comparison of expected acceptance with actual acceptance by trade unions, employers and employees for all trainees*

Expected / Actual	Trade unions		Employers		Employees	
	Pessimists	Optimists	Pessimists	Optimists	Pessimists	Optimists
Very good	7	76	7	132	16	127
	63.6	*62.3*	*63.6*	*58.7*	*64.0*	*60.2*
Good	3	39	3	71	8	63
	27.3	*32.0*	*27.3*	*31.6*	*32.0*	*29.9*
Poor	1	5	1	21	1	18
	9.1	*4.1*	*9.1*	*9.3*	*4.0*	*8.5*
Not at all	—	2	—	1	—	3
		1.6		*0.4*		*1.4*
TOTAL N =	11	122	11	225	25	211
% =	*100.0*	*100.0*	*100.0*	*100.0*	*100.0*	*100.0*
Don't know	—	8	3	16	3	16
N/a [a]	13	103	1	1	1	1
TOTAL N =	24	233	15	242	29	228

Note: These figures total only 257 instead of 258 because one man never worked.

[a] See Table 9.12, note a.

rating of their acceptance by employers, unions and employees in the light of how they expected to be received when they completed training. In the initial questionnaire, trainees were asked if they expected to be accepted as skilled by each of the three groups, and their answers are compared with their actual situation in Table 9.13.

There are no significant differences between those who did not think that they would be accepted as skilled (pessimists) and the others (optimists) in their assessment of their actual situation. The only obvious difference is that there are fewer men who always used their skill in the first group; comparisons are difficult due to the small numbers and this difference is only significant at the 10 per cent level for those who did not expect acceptance from employers. It may be that at least some of the people who did not expect to be accepted as skilled men at work were more sensitive to any criticism or resistance than others who were not expecting any antagonism, and quite likely the self-fulfilling prophecy is at work here. But clearly, the number of original 'pessimists' is small, and this is hardly surprising, given that all trainees were in the final analysis volunteers, and relatively few pessimists are likely to volunteer for training.

CONCLUSION

To conclude, there certainly was some resistance to the trainees, and all sectors of industry are 'guilty' to a greater or lesser extent. The magnitude of such resistance is, however, difficult to judge with any degree of precision due to the conflicting reports from union representatives, from employers and not least of all from the trainees. It is reasonably safe to assume that the actual or perceived existence of this resistance is one factor in deciding some trainees to abandon their new skill. The majority of trainees, however, experienced or perceived little resistance to dilution, and this is probably the most significant result obtained from this part of the exercise; no doubt this lack of resistance contributed greatly to the high success rate of the trainees in establishing themselves as members of the skilled work-force, and this is perhaps surprising. For given the traditions of our skilled workers and their trade unions, the often supposed rigidity with which 'skilled unions' are expected to exercise their control function, and the inescapable fact that employers, too, have been socialised in this industrial *milieu*, one may be excused for anticipating a rather different result.

Chapter 10

The Social Mobility
of a Group of Trainees

A whole host of surveys has indicated that a clear correlation between job and prestige exists.[1] This being so, it could be assumed that the acquisition of a higher skill would give the trainees higher prestige and that this may in turn be perceived in terms of upward social mobility. As has been shown in the foregoing, only a relatively small proportion of trainees gave the anticipation of 'higher social status' as the main motivating factor for seeking training, yet the following will indicate that many more than those who did so claimed in one way or another to have climbed the social ladder once they had been accepted as skilled men.

For the layman the concept of social class is usually a very simple one, but for the sociologist with his demand for precision of definitions it is anything but that; social stratification is a complex phenomenon.

Max Weber,[2] in keeping with the tradition of European sociology, maintained that the *economic* organisation of a society is a basis of social stratification. Now whilst income is one way of ranking people, it is patently deficient in a number of ways; for example assembly workers can (and often do) outearn small shopkeepers. Thus Weber specified the *source* of income as a criterion in the ranking process; i.e. what people do in the division of labour or what they own as well as what they earn gives a more complete picture of stratification in economic terms. And for Weber, as for Karl Marx, property and lack of property are the basic categories of all class situations.

Status and class are now not synonymous, for status refers to the ranking of social groups by prestige and honour. A status group exists when a number of persons occupy a similar position in the prestige ranking in a given community, when they recognise each other as equals and finally when they regularly interact with each other, i.e. when they exhibit a common style of life.

---

[1] See for example, J. Hall and D. C. Jones, 'Social Grading of Occupations', *British Journal of Sociology*, Vol. 1 (1950), pp. 31–55; and D. V. Glass (ed.), *Social Mobility in Britain* (Routledge, 1954).

[2] Max Weber, 'Class Status and Party', in H. Gerth and C. Wright Mills, *From Max Weber: Essays in Sociology* (Oxford University Press, 1946), pp. 180–95.

If we now refer to Chapter 1 of this volume, when the work of Lockwood was quoted [3] it will be observed that 'market' and 'work' situations are manifestations of social class, whilst the status situation must stand on its own in so far as it is possible to have a number of disparate status groups within a social class.

Most of the foregoing in this book so far has dealt with the market situation of trainees, i.e. with wages, security and the like. Implicitly it has also dealt with the work situation of trainees; patently many craftsmen have a fair measure of autonomy whilst at work, a situation denied to the majority of the less skilled workers. Supervision is not so strict in general, as the skilled man is supposed to possess a degree of expertise which makes this unnecessary. This chapter, then, will deal in the main with the status implications of acquiring a skill, as opposed to problems of work and market conditions which were previously dealt with. It must, however, be noted, as Lockwood so clearly perceived,[4] 'class and status are not alternative, but complementary viewpoints of the reality of any given stratification system'. And again,[5] 'Class focuses on the divisions which result from the brute facts of economic organisation. Status relates to the more subtle distinctions which stem from the values that men set on each other's activities.' These points are emphasised by Giddens [6] when he writes that 'far from becoming increasingly homogeneous, the working class has become diversified: the differences in skill level serve as a basis for divisions of interest which cut across the unity of the class as a whole'. This is of course in keeping with the above, for [7] 'as Weber indicates, possession of recognised skills . . . is the major factor influencing market capacity'.

The previous chapters of this book will have indicated that in terms of market conditions (and probably in terms of work conditions also) the trainees have, by-and-large, profited. The status element must now be analysed. Yet the status element has a number of dimensions. Status must be assumed by the holder, but it must also be accorded by others. And status is likely to have outward indications also. Writing of white-collar workers, Allen [8] maintained that because the status of such workers has depended largely on their ability to engage in selective consumption, anything reducing purchasing-power has status implications. If Allen is right then it follows that the ability to engage in increased 'selective consumption' (e.g. the acquisition of a colour television set or a washing machine) should also have status implications. It was one of the objectives of the longitudinal research project to establish to what extent, if any, selective consumption after the training period would manifest itself.

[3] D. Lockwood, *The Blackcoated Worker* (Allen & Unwin, 1958).

[4] *ibid.*, p. 202n.

[5] *ibid.*, p. 208.

[6] A. Giddens, *The Class Structure of Advanced Societies* (Hutchinson, 1973), p. 55.

[7] *ibid.*, p. 103.

[8] V. L. Allen, *The Sociology of Industrial Relations* (Longman, 1971).

Although the following looks in some detail at a number of status factors, the assessment of social-status change with skills acquisition was only one of a number of facts which the longitudinal research project sought to establish. Yet change in status can be very significant to the person involved and not infrequently so to the remainder of society. And status is closely interwoven with skill. Thus [9] 'every trade or . . . profession has always had an interest in making its labour scarce so as to get a better price for it, but Craft Societies' motivation for control run deeper than this. It was essentially protective . . . of its status as well as standards'. What was true of craft societies then is no doubt also true of craft practitioners now: skill, provided it is kept in sufficiently short supply so as not to flood the market, is likely to grant status. Perhaps the case of an apprentice, much quoted in 1970, who was sacked by his employer for below-par performance at his technical college exams makes this point. It went to appeal, when (the then) Mr Justice Widgery, in finding for the dismissed apprentice, maintained that 'an apprenticeship contract secures three things for the apprentice: the instruction and training to acquire skills which will be of value to him for the rest of his life; the *status* [our italics] conferred on a young man who completes his apprenticeship . . . and a money payment during the period of the apprenticeship itself'.[10] The apprentice in question obtained 'damages' over and above those paid in the past, in that he was compensated for loss of status.[11]

If an apprenticeship brings status, a government training centre course should be likewise, providing the trainee is accepted eventually as a skilled man. The trainees certainly appeared to know what the agents of status-classification were; they generally agreed that people who share similar positions in the prestige hierarchy tend to share a common life-style in terms of dress, manners, speech, consumption patterns, use of leisure and the like.[12]

This chapter, then, deals with that part of the research project which is concerned with the question of social mobility of the trainees following their training. It indicates that there is still an awareness of the existence of a class structure in this country among working people and suggests that the majority of manual workers perceive themselves as belonging to the working class. The hypothesis that semi-skilled and unskilled workers who apply for government training centre courses are frequently motivated to do so in order to gain higher status is examined. One assumption at the outset of the project was that some men would experience feelings of 'relative deprivation' in that they had 'reference groups' of skilled workers with whom they compared themselves and in so doing they would feel

---

[9] A. Flanders, *Trade Unions and the Force of Tradition* (University of Southampton, 1969), p. 11.

[10] See for example 'Diogenes on Law', *New Society* (7 May 1970).

[11] Ewan Mitchell, 'Sacking Your Apprentice', *Personnel Management* (August 1970).

[12] Bredemeier and Stephenson, *The Analysis of Social Systems* (Holt, Rinehart & Winston, 1970), p. 319.

themselves to be inferior.[13] It was further assumed that in order to remedy this situation the trainees would seek to join the ranks of skilled men by volunteering for training. If this hypothesis is correct, then some degree of upward social mobility should be discernible amongst the trainees in the post-training period. In order to verify – or reject – the general hypothesis, trainees and control groups were asked to rate themselves within the class structure at the beginning and end of the research, a period separated by eighteen months of time. As the term 'status' has little meaning to the layman, as always in such instances the words 'social class' were used when status questions were asked. The various groups were also asked to answer a number of questions from which some objective appraisal of social mobility could be made.

More specifically, measurement of social mobility was attempted on:

1. *Subjective assessment:* trainees, unemployed and operator control groups were asked at the beginning and end of the survey period to rate themselves on a six-point scale ranging from upper middle class to lower working class, corresponding to the frequently used classification A, B, C_1, C_2, D and E. Craftsmen and apprentices were asked the same question only on the final questionnaire.

2. *Objective assessment:* members of the sample of trainees were asked various questions on ownership of household durables and the like, on types of housing and on newspaper readership. Operators and unemployed were asked questions similar to those put to the trainees at the beginning and end of the research, but craftsmen and apprentices were asked this at the end of the period only. Additional to the comparisons offered by control groups, an attempt was made to use national studies of readership and ownership patterns related to 'social class', but regional differences limited their usefulness. Also, the scale of these surveys was not sufficiently accurate to measure the very fine changes expected in this survey.

The following discussion on the social mobility of the trainees depends to a great extent on the comparison between that group and the various control groups. As these control groups were wholly Scottish and only like

[13] See W. G. Runciman, *Relative Deprivation and Social Justice* (Penguin, 1966). Runciman claims that 'relative deprivation should always be understood to mean a sense of deprivation; a person who is "relatively deprived" need not be "objectively" deprived in the more usual sense that he is demonstrably lacking something. In addition, relative deprivation means that the sense of deprivation is such as to involve a comparison with an imagined situation of some other person or group. The other person or group is the "reference group" or more accurately "comparative reference group"' (pp. 11–12). Naturally, the reference group for our trainees must have consisted of skilled men with whom the majority came into regular contact and this contact must have activated feelings of relative deprivation. Early discussions with many of the trainees indicated that the foregoing had in fact been experienced by many of the trainees, and especially by those who volunteered for training whilst in employment.

and like should be compared, the social mobility of the Liverpool trainees is not considered. The term 'trainee' throughout this chapter will therefore refer to the Scottish trainees only.

1. SUBJECTIVE RATING

Subjective rating deals with people locating themselves in a structure and is therefore a question of self-assessment. Richard Centers [14] reserved the term 'social class', which he regards as a psychological phenomenon, to subjective criteria of stratification. It is not intended to so limit the use of the term, but the significance of subjective aspects cannot be overemphasised. It is therefore intended to deal in some depth with the subjective views of trainees and of control groups.

From the 258 trainees who made up the final sample of the research, 25 had to be discarded as they failed to answer the pertinent questions on the initial or final questionnaire or on both. The 233 trainees who remained were divided thus:

(*a*) *upwardly mobile* – those whose final self-rating in the social scale was higher than their initial rating;

(*b*) *downwardly mobile* – those whose final self-rating in the social scale was lower than their initial rating;

(*c*) *immobile* – those whose final self-rating in the social scale was the same as their initial rating.

Common sense indicates that there should be a high degree of upward mobility among those trainees who, after leaving the training centre, have always been employed in jobs where they used their skills. Table 10.1 does in fact indicate that this was so in that a disproportionately high number of upwardly mobile men in Scotland belong to group A.

It will be noted that some of group A have moved down whilst some of groups B and C have moved up – an analysis of the background and circumstances of these men gives a clue as to why they should move in the direction opposite to that which was anticipated. Thus 15 men in group A moved down; it would appear that some of these men had experiences which gave them feelings of second-class citizenship – comments here such as 'trainees are cheap labour' were indicative of this. And 3 men here were unemployed when they completed their final questionnaire; Centers holds that unemployment will make a man rate himself low on the social scale.

Twelve men in groups B and C moved up the social scale according to their own view. One man ended up a supervisor, another was self-employed, so it is easy to speculate why they moved up, as is the case of those in group B who were using their skill at the end of the survey period. And 5 men who were unemployed when they volunteered for a government training centre course were now in employment. Whilst not all unexpected moves

[14] R. Centers, *The Social Psychology of Class* (Princeton University Press, 1949).

can be accounted for in this way, enough data are available to indicate that in general an apparent move in the 'wrong' direction most often has a rational explanation.

TABLE 10.1　*Degree of mobility among trainees according to their post-training employment*

Social mobility

Employment situation of trainees	Upward	Immobile	Downward	Total N =	Don't know
A	59	90	15	164	13
	36.0	*54.9*	*9.2*	*100.1*	
B	4	33	8	45	7
	8.9	*73.3*	*17.8*	*100.0*	
C	8	13	3	24	5
	33.3	*54.2*	*12.5*	*100.0*	
TOTAL	71	136	26	233	25
	30.5	*58.4*	*11.2*	*100.1*	

Note: Throughout the chapter figures in italics in the tables indicate percentages.

A Those who used their skill in all jobs.

B Those who used their skill some of the time.

C Those who never used their skill.

Considering now the group B members who moved down – 8 out of 45 compared with 15 out of 164 in group A – this is to be expected, as those who have used their skill in the past but do not use it now are likely to suffer a great disappointment which should have an effect on their subjective judgement of their position in the social prestige hierarchy.

It may now be useful to consider the operators and unemployed control groups and compare their mobility with that of the trainees – for if such upward mobility as has been ascertained among the trainees is due to their new skills, then there should be a significant difference in the upward mobility of the trainees and of these two control groups. That this is in fact so is indicated by Table 10.2.

TABLE 10.2　*Social mobility of trainees, operators and unemployed*

	Social mobility				
	Upward	Immobile	Downward	Total	Don't know
Trainees	71	136	26	233	25
	30.5	*58.4*	*11.2*	*100.1*	
Operators and unemployed	43	117	17	177	
	24.3	*66.1*	*9.6*	*100.0*	

On the face of it an excessive number of operators and unemployed men are upwardly mobile but their changed circumstances have to be taken into account. Thus 20 unemployed men were 'upwardly mobile' – but 18 of these had regular employment at the end of the research period, and of the 23 operators who claimed upward mobility, 8 had obtained either better jobs or promotion in the intervening period.

Some downward mobility has to be expected, but its causes should make sense. This in fact many do if the individual cases are analysed. Some claims of downward mobility made good sense, for example of the 7 unemployed men who were socially downwardly mobile, 2 were still unemployed at the end of the eighteen-month period and 2 were in jobs of lower status than their last job prior to the initial unemployment.

In general it may be hypothesised that the trainees' distribution in their social hierarchy at the beginning of the research should resemble that of the operators and the unemployed, and at the end of the exercise social mobility should have taken place so that the trainees should now in the main resemble the craftsmen and ex-apprentices. Table 10.3 gives the before-and-after picture. There are no significant differences in the proportion of trainees and control groups who claim to be upper working class or higher at the beginning of the research; at the end of the period a hierarchy of status claims, however, becomes apparent (see Table 10.4).

It is also possible to construct a table in terms of three groups only: 'traditional craftsmen' (craftsmen and apprentices); trainees, and 'not skilled' (operators and unemployed, since few if any of the unemployed made much claim to skill) – see Table 10.5.

TABLE 10.3   *Self-rating of position in the social hierarchy at the beginning and end of the research period*

(a) Initially	Lower middle and higher	Upper working	Working	Lower working	Total	Don't know
Trainees	14	46	169	4	233	25
	6.0	*19.7*	*72.5*	*1.7*	*99.9*	
Operators	9	11	69	1	90	6
	10.0	*12.2*	*76.7*	*1.1*	*99.9*	
Unemployed	2	10	65	10	87	6
	2.3	*11.5*	*74.7*	*11.5*	*100.0*	
(b) Finally						
Trainees	28	72	130	3	233	25
	12.0	*30.9*	*55.8*	*1.3*	*100.0*	
Operators	11	19	59	1	90	6
	12.2	*21.1*	*65.6*	*1.1*	*100.0*	
Unemployed	8	13	62	4	87	6
	9.2	*14.9*	*71.3*	*4.6*	*100.0*	
Craftsmen	14	30	39	1	84	12
	16.7	*35.7*	*46.4*	*1.2*	*100.0*	
Apprentices	21	33	42	—	96	4
	21.9	*34.4*	*43.8*		*100.1*	

TABLE 10.4   *Numbers and percentages of various groups who rated them-*
selves upper working class or higher at the end of the
research period

Apprentices	*Craftsmen*	*Trainees*	*Operators*	*Unemployed*
N = 96	84	233	90	87
% = 56.3	52.4	42.9	33.3	24.1

TABLE 10.5   *Self-rating of trainees and control groups at end of survey*

	Upper working class or higher	*Working class or lower*	*Total*	*Don't know*
Traditional	98	82	180	16
craftsmen	*54.4*	*45.6*	*100.0*	
Trainees	100	133	233	25
	42.9	*57.1*	*100.0*	
Not skilled	51	126	177	12
	28.8	*71.2*	*100.0*	

The difference between the trainees and the unskilled control groups on the
issue of self-rating was not highly significant initially ($p < .10$). At the end
of the survey period, however, this difference had become highly significant
($p < .005$), which indicates that the trainees have moved away from the
operator and unemployed groups and towards the men in the craftsmen
and apprentice groups. This movement was not completed, however, in
that the trainees had not, at the end of the survey period, caught up with the
craftsmen and apprentices in the subjective assessment of their assumed
new status.

During the pilot stage of the research project it was found that a small
minority of trainees were not anxious to rate themselves on the social
scale if the question came out of the blue. It was therefore decided to
precede this question with one or two others which would get the respondent used to the idea that questions relating to social class and social status
were being asked. No difficulties of any kind were thereafter experienced
in getting the trainees – or any other group – to complete the self-rating
section in the questionnaire.

The first question was: 'Do you think that social class is still an important factor in the life of contemporary Britain?' The second question asked
respondents to tick, from a list of eight – itself established from a more
extensive pilot list – all the factors which they thought important in determining a person's 'position in the class structure' (see Table 10.6).

It is interesting, though perhaps not surprising, to note that in a society
making some pretence – albeit only a limited one – of 'openness', almost
three-quarters (70.0 per cent) of these men should still feel that class is of
importance in Britain. The trainees were the most 'class-conscious' group –

which again emphasises the motivational aspect of an awareness of class structure coupled with a knowledge of one's own lowly status in motivating at least some of them to 'improve' their situation.

TABLE 10.6   *Do you think that social class is still an important factor in the life of contemporary Britain?*

	Scottish trainees	Liverpool trainees	Operators	Unemployed
	%	%	%	%
Yes	75.2	72.7	64.6	60.2
No	24.0	27.3	31.3	33.3
Don't know	0.8	—	4.2	6.5
TOTAL N =	258	33	96	93
% =	100.0	100.0	100.1	100.0

The second 'lead-in' question asked for factors of importance in determining social class. Although 24 per cent of the trainees had said that they did not believe that class was important, only 5 men (1.9 per cent) continued the argument to say that as there was no importance in class there were no factors governing class; all other trainees listed the factors which they considered important. A similar pattern repeated itself with the other groups which answered this question. Table 10.7 gives the results of this question.

TABLE 10.7   *Important factors determining social class position* (%)

Placing	Scotland N = 258	Liverpool N = 33	Operators N = 96	Unemployed N = 93
1st	Education 77.9	Education 90.9	Education 85.4	Education 86.0
2nd	Occupation 64.0	Property 72.7	Income 69.8	Income 78.5
3rd	Income 62.4	Occupation 66.7	Occupation 62.5	Occupation 57.0
4th	Property 43.0	Birth 57.6	Speech 47.9	Speech 38.7
5th	Birth 41.9	Income 54.5	Dress 41.7	Property 35.5
6th	Speech 38.8	Speech [a] 21.2	Property 40.6	Birth 33.3
7th	Dress 20.5	Expenditure [a] 21.2	Birth 28.1	Dress 30.1
8th	Expenditure 17.4	Dress 18.2	Expenditure 21.9	Expenditure 16.1

[a] 6th equal.

Undoubtedly, education was regarded as most important by all groups; the 'Liverpudlians' were the most certain that it was education which counted in placing a person in the class structure, despite the traditional view that all Scots place a high premium on education. Occupation came second for the Scottish trainees, which is to be expected when they are spending so much time improving their own occupational prospects. For the Liverpool group, which was expected to have similar opinions, occupation slid to third place, ousted by property; this is obviously a result of the much higher level of home ownership in England.

It is not surprising that income came high on the list for operators and unemployed. Many operators are in jobs where money is the only satisfaction to be obtained from the job and the only advancement which they can expect will be in terms of higher wages, i.e. where an 'instrumental' attitude towards work can be expected. And the unemployed as a group must be only too well aware that they have no earned income.

2. SUBJECTIVE/OBJECTIVE RATING

Housing fell into a combined subjective and objective assessment classification, in that the questions on housing asked firstly the type of housing the respondent was living in at the time – an objective (i.e. factual) criterion – and then the type of housing he would like to live in, which is of course a subjective question.

The purpose of the question was to measure social mobility in two ways. Firstly, it was assumed that when a person who previously rented a council house or a private house sets out to become an owner-occupier, then some measure of upward social mobility has taken place; and when a person who is an owner-occupier sets out to change to rented accommodation then downward social mobility is assumed to have taken place. Similarly, on the subjective or attitudinal level, when a person who previously wished to rent accommodation now desires to become an owner-occupier, upward social mobility is assumed to have taken place, and alternatively, when a person who previously wished for owner-occupation now desires to rent, downward social mobility is assumed. Unfortunately, this measure is not as fine as one would like it to be, due to the unique housing situation in Scotland with its tradition of heavily subsidised local authority housing, which makes owner-occupation among the manual working classes a relative rarity. Accepting Richard Hoggart's view [15] that different streets and houses in working-class areas have differing amounts of prestige, social mobility probably takes place within the local authority estates, but cost and time made it impossible for us to measure this. The legacy of cheap local authority housing appeared then to be in jeopardy, with the rapid increases in council house rents, but no discernible significant move into private-sector housing among working-class Scots was found, as Table 10.8 illustrates.

[15] R. Hoggart, *The Uses of Literature* (Chatto & Windus, 1957).

TABLE 10.8   *Actual housing situation at beginning and end of research period*

(a) *At beginning of research*

Type of housing	Trainees	Craftsmen	Operators	Unemployed
	%	%	%	%
Owner-occupier	11.6	—	18.8	9.7
Rent private	10.1	—	4.2	1.1
Rent council	55.4	—	54.2	68.8
In digs [a]	19.4	—	22.9	20.4
Don't know	3.5	—	—	—
TOTAL N =	258	—	96	93
% =	100.0	—	100.1	100.0

(b) *At end of research*

Owner-occupier	11.6	25.0	16.7	8.6
Rent private	7.4	7.3	4.2	1.1
Rent council	60.9	55.2	55.2	71.0
In digs	19.8	12.5	17.7	19.4
Don't know	0.4	—	6.3	—
TOTAL N =	258	96	96	93
% =	100.1	100.0	100.1	100.1

[a] 'In digs' includes trainees who lived with friends and relatives; they may have been married or single, but were not heads of households.

From Table 10.8 it will be noted that at the end of the research period more trainees – and to a lesser extent other groups – lived in council houses. Two reasons account for this: fewer men were now renting from private landlords – which may possibly be viewed as at least some measure of upward mobility – and the number of uncompleted questions was lower. As regards house ownership, this had remained stable for the trainees, whilst the proportion of operators and unemployed owning or buying a house had diminished, so that in this respect at least the trainees had gained some relative 'advantage'. Regarding the lack of absolute mobility in housing, it may be that an eighteen-month period is not long enough to provide a meaningful measure; time is needed to obtain a job and acquire sufficient capital in order to raise a mortgage. Building society limitations on lending to people with low incomes cannot be ignored and the income data of the trainees indicate that their incomes were relatively low when first they left their training centres. The eighteen-month period may not have been sufficient to get the trainees for long enough into the higher earning league.

A measure which acts more immediately and is more meaningful for our purpose is the type of housing which is desired at the beginning and end of the research period, for this is a subjective assessment which is at least independent of short-term economic effects. Table 10.9, which shows the desired housing of all pertinent groups at the beginning and end of the survey, indicates that despite the large proportion of all groups who lived in council housing only relatively few claimed they desired to do so.

TABLE 10.9   *Desired housing at the beginning and end of the research period*

(a) *At the beginning of the research*

Type of housing	Trainees	Craftsmen	Operators	Unemployed
	%	%	%	%
Owner-occupier	75.2	—	78.1	73.1
Rent privately	1.6	—	2.1	—
Rent council	16.7	—	18.8	20.4
In digs	—	—	—	—
Don't know	6.6	—	1.0	6.5
TOTAL N =	258	—	96	93
% =	100.1	—	100.0	100,0

(b) *At the end of the research*

Owner-occupier	81.8	86.5	86.5	80.6
Rent privately	3.5	1.0	1.0	1.1
Rent council	12.0	10.4	10.4	15.1
In digs	1.2	1.0	1.0	3.2
Don't know	1.6	1.0	1.0	—
TOTAL N =	258	96	96	93
% =	100.1	99.9	99.9	100.0

At the beginning of the research period the trainees were least likely to prefer renting a council house, whilst the unemployed were the most likely to prefer this type of housing – which is very much as expected. It will be noted that at the end of the survey period all groups had reduced their desire to rent a council house; how much of this was due to upward social mobility of all the groups and how much was due to the continuing rise in council rents is, however, difficult to judge. As regards desired owner-occupation, all groups showed 'upward social mobility' on the assumption that owner-occupation rates higher than renting. One is, however, well aware that for some persons owner-occupation is not preferred for a whole host of reasons, such as having to leave one's friends and relations, going in for 'unnecessary' social pretence, and so on. In general, however, we would argue that owner-occupation in this country is of higher prestige for almost all sectors of society than is renting.

At the end of the period, then, the trainees were a little ahead of the unemployed, but behind the craftsmen and the operators. These changes in desired housing are not sufficiently great to give a clear indication of 'subjective social mobility'. The conclusion here mirrors that on actual housing, in that our eighteen-month period may simply not be long enough to allow trainees to catch up on the traditional craftsmen.

3. OBJECTIVE RATING

Objective rating deals with people in a social structure, and to that extent can be fairly independent of the person's perception of his situation. Objective social mobility deals with structural change. Yet even here subjectivity is seldom completely absent. Thus in an acquisitive society in which the phrase 'keeping up with the Joneses' has become part of common speech, it would be expected that trainees attempting to move up the social ladder would try to demonstrate their new status by gathering household goods and leisure commodities appropriate to their new position. It could of course be objected that any increase in ownership was the result solely of higher wages and increased purchasing power; yet the previous discussion on trainees' wages suggests that any gains in trainees' earnings were not sufficiently great, in comparison with gains in earnings of control groups, to account for the greater amount of purchasing which took place. Thus whilst market relations may be of significance here, questions of social status are likely to be more significant.

The list of possessions about which the samples were asked is given in Table 10.10. The trainees acquired between them 143 new pieces of hardware during the eighteen-month period, giving an average rate of 0.55 pieces per man, as compared with an average acquisition of 0.39 pieces per man for operators, craftsmen and unemployed. All this does not, however, take into account such variables as age, marital status, and geographical mobility; additionally it is patently unrealistic to compare the purchase of a cheap camera with that of, say, a medium-priced car. Yet it does seem that the trainees had in fact done more shopping than any of the other groups during the eighteen-month period. This may of course be in part due to hire purchase companies' attitudes to lending to trainees undergoing training; these companies appear to regard an ex-trainee's new earnings more favourably than they would a training allowance. Despite this, some of the differences are likely to be due to some measure of upward social mobility in terms of Allen's 'selective consumption'.[16] This assumes that the ownership of these goods does indicate such mobility.

Table 10.10 shows gains in ownership of the commodities in question.

On the final questionnaire the trainees and all the control groups were asked if they had owned eighteen months previously, and if they owned now, any of the articles quoted in Table 10.10. It was therefore possible to establish how many of the men had always owned, had purchased or had disposed of any of the articles. For fairly obvious reasons the apprentices were ignored: the majority of them were not married and changes which occurred when men in this group obtained new possessions were nearly always major ones due to marriage.

The assumption which gave rise to this part of the investigation was that

[16] V. L. Allen, op. cit.

TABLE 10.10   *Gains in ownership for all groups*

Commodity	Trainees	Craftsmen	Operators	Unemployed	Total controls
Car	24	5	5	4	14
	9.3	*5.2*	*5.2*	*4.3*	
Telephone	15	8	7	1	16
	5.8	*8.3*	*7.3*	*1.1*	
Washing machine	31	3	11	5	19
	12.0	*3.1*	*11.5*	*5.4*	
Fridge	22	3	7	5	15
	8.5	*3.1*	*7.3*	*5.4*	
Deep freeze	3	2	1	2	5
	1.2	*2.1*	*1.0*	*2.2*	
Television	10	2	6	2	10
	3.9	*2.1*	*6.3*	*2.2*	
Vacuum cleaner	20	—	5	1	6
	7.8		*5.2*	*1.1*	
Dishwasher	—	2	1	—	3
		2.1	*1.0*		
Food mixer	9	8	3	1	12
	3.5	*8.3*	*3.1*	*1.1*	
Camera	9	2	6	1	9
	3.5	*2.1*	*6.3*	*1.1*	

TOTAL NUMBER OF ARTICLES OBTAINED					
N = 143	35	52	22	109
% = *55.4*	*36.5*	*54.2*	*23.7*	*38.5*
N = 258	96	96	93	285

before training the trainees' possessions would be similar to those owned by the operators and unemployed; after training, however, the things which they owned would tend to be more akin to those of the craftsmen, as selective consumption for the purpose of status elevation – though not for that alone – took place.

For purposes of analysis, the following articles only will now be considered in the main, so as to add clarity and to simplify: cars, washing machines, vacuum cleaners and cameras. The first may be viewed as a family – or in the case of a single man, a private – luxury item. The second and third are household durables which are not nowadays seen as luxuries; the fourth is again a luxury item, although here an added complication arises, in that a camera can be relatively cheap or very expensive. This last point is, however, equally true for trainees and control groups, which should to some extent at least have a cancelling effect.

If one considers age as a variable, then the effects of this on ownership can be demonstrated (see Table 10.11). It will be noted that the ownership of luxury items is fairly independent of age, but that older trainees were more likely to possess household durables; this is, of course, to be expected, for the 'younger' group contains the majority of the single men, and the 'older' married man is more likely to possess a large number of household durables than his younger counterpart.

TABLE 10.11   *Age versus ownership for trainees at the end of the research period*

Commodity	Under 35 years old			Over 35 years old		
	Owner	Non-owner	Total	Owner	Non-owner	Total
Car	76	100	176	35	47	82
	43.2	56.8	100.0	42.7	57.3	100.0
Washing machine	117	59	176	60	22	82
	66.5	33.5	100.0	73.2	26.8	100.0
Vacuum cleaner	120	56	176	69	13	82
	68.2	31.8	100.0	84.1	15.9	100.0
Refrigerator	57	119	176	40	42	82
	32.4	67.6	100.0	48.8	51.2	100.0
Camera	126	50	176	54	28	82
	71.6	28.4	100.0	65.9	34.1	100.0

Comparing car ownership of the two groups, the difference is not statistically significant, which is hardly surprising, for in contempoary Britain car ownership appears to be independent of age (above a certain minimum) and of marital status. For washing machines the observed chi-square value was not statistically significant, i.e. ownership cannot be linked to age; it may be that a washing machine is one of the first household durables bought by newly-weds. Vacuum cleaner ownership difference was, however, statistically significant; possibly newly-weds do not possess enough carpets to make the ownership of a cleaner a pressing necessity. Refrigerator ownership was again linked to age; it may be that these items are only bought after more pressing needs – for example for cars and washing machines – are met. Finally the difference in camera ownership for the two groups was not statistically significant; like cars, cameras appear to be viewed as highly desirable luxury items.

Age is of course not the only variable of interest, and Table 10.12 indicates the final ownership, at the end of the research period, of cars, washing machines, vacuum cleaners and cameras for all groups. An analysis on the basis of ownership of the four items is now possible; once again it must be emphasised that for obvious reasons the apprentices make a poor control group.

(a) *Car Ownership*
Comparing the trainees with the craftsmen, a significant difference was observed, and this was also true when the comparison was made between

the trainees and the operators and unemployed. Thus for car ownership the trainees at the end of the survey period were above the operators and unemployed but below the craftsmen.

TABLE 10.12 *Ownership of four commodities for all groups at end of survey*

	Car	Washing machine	Vacuum cleaner	Camera
Trainees [a]	87	146	169	171
N = 258	33.7	56.0	65.6	66.4
[b]	24	31	20	9
	9.3	12.0	7.8	3.5
Craftsmen [a]	56	74	81	78
N = 96	58.3	77.1	84.4	81.3
[b]	5	3	—	2
	5.2	3.1		2.1
Apprentices [a]	30	28	30	65
N = 100	30.0	28.0	30.0	65.0
[b]	11	9	10	10
	11.0	9.0	10.0	10.0
Operators [a]	21	47	66	53
N = 96	21.9	49.0	68.8	55.2
[b]	5	11	5	6
	5.2	11.5	5.2	6.3
Unemployed [a]	9	31	45	48
N = 93	9.7	33.3	48.4	51.6
[b]	4	5	1	1
	4.3	5.4	1.1	1.1

[a] owned at beginning and end of survey

[b] did not own at beginning but owned at end of survey, i.e. bought during research period.

(b) *Washing Machine Ownership*
Comparing trainees with operators and unemployed a statistically significant difference was observed and this was equally true when the trainees were compared with the craftsmen. Thus for washing machine ownership the trainees were above the operators and unemployed but below the craftsmen at the end of the survey period.

(c) *Vacuum Cleaner Ownership*
The trainees were here found at the end of the survey period to be above the operators and unemployed but again below the craftsmen.

(d) *Camera Ownership*
Here the trainees were, at the end of the research period, found to be above the operators and unemployed but once again below the craftsmen.

To sum this section up, it may be stated that the trainees had left the control groups of operators and unemployed – from whence they originated – behind, but had not yet reached the level of the craftsmen. They therefore occupy an intermediary position, which one would expect them to. Presumably the timespan of the research was too short for the process to be completed. So the trainees own proportionally more of each commodity than do the operators and unemployed groups, but still lag behind the craftsmen. To complicate the situation, it was found that this was to a lesser extent also true at the beginning of the research period, and this presents the problem of why the trainees should be so different at the beginning of the research period from the two groups whom they were supposed to resemble. The answer here must surely be that the trainees were significantly different from their 'peers' before they went forward for training, and that these differences may in fact have contributed to their decision to train. It may be thought that this assumption would be easier to accept were the trainees superior to the operators and unemployed control groups in all objective aspects, yet this is not so, for they fall behind the operators in housing, as was indicated in the foregoing. The only explanation for this must hinge on the relative unimportance of house ownership in Scotland. It would appear that the relevant reference group had made its pressure felt to many trainees prior to training, that feelings of relative deprivation were very much perceived by these and that selective consumption had already been engaged in and had merely been indulged in more fully as the higher wages of skilled men became nearer to reality for the ex-trainee.

NEWSPAPER READERSHIP

Newspaper readership may be viewed as another objective tool for measuring social mobility. Different daily and Sunday newspapers are aimed at different parts of the market according to social class. Thus the 'quality' press is written in the main for members of socio-economic classes A and B and to a lesser extent for C_1, whilst the 'popular' press is aimed mainly at social classes C_2, D and E. Advertisers take the class mix of newspaper readers into account; thus for example advertisements of vacancies for professional jobs will be inserted in the quality press.

It was assumed that changes in newspaper reading habits over the period of our research by the trainees would act as an indicator of social mobility; this they did but only to a very limited extent. It was of course accepted from the outset that any upward social mobility would be of a limited nature only, for example from social class D (semi- and unskilled) to C_2 (skilled manual) and would not show up easily in terms of newspaper readership. It could not possibly be expected that there would be a mass transfer from the popular press to quality newspapers. Nor was it expected that accurate data would be available from external sources to differentiate newspaper readership on a class basis in east Scotland. The differences in regional and area readership proved, however, to be rather larger than was anticipated, and this made data obtained from other sources useless for the purpose of this research; hence all controls had to be built into the research project itself. Initially no questions on social class were asked of the craftsmen and apprentices, but with the mounting problems of obtaining control data external to the project it became apparent that these two groups would have to act as controls, and in the final questionnaire the questions on 'social class' were put to the craftsmen and apprentices groups as well as to the other controls. Retrospectively, it would have been useful to have obtained data on newspaper readership patterns from the craftsmen and apprentices at the beginning of the research period. Newspaper readership of all the groups at the completion of the research is known (see Tables 10.13 and 10.14).

In attempting to monitor changes in newspaper readership patterns due to intragenerational social mobility of such a limited nature as this project was likely to produce, we were of course well aware that changes in readership patterns were likely to be of a very limited nature themselves – as indeed proved to be the case. Yet changes in readership patterns did take place, and given the limited nature of the social mobility observed, the changes in readership patterns were certainly as significant as one could possibly hope for.

Table 10.13 indicates some movement in the daily newspaper readership pattern during the period of the project, providing a clue that a somewhat more sophisticated type of newspaper readership was being established by the trainees. Thus the readership of the *Daily Record* (the Scottish equivalent of the English *Daily Mirror*) dropped from 42.2 per cent of the trainees to 38.0 per cent. The fact that only 21.9 per cent of craftsmen read this paper, whilst at the same time 43.0 per cent of the unemployed did so, gives some indication of the 'class' basis of readership of this paper. The movement here is as expected. The timespan of the research project is once again a limiting factor here.

Sunday newspaper readership indicates a trend similar to that of daily newspapers. Thus, for example, at the start of the project period 65.5 per cent of the trainees read the *Sunday Post*, a figure which dropped to 60.1 per cent by the end of the research; for purposes of comparison it will be noted that at the end of the research period 57.3 per cent of the craftsmen, 68.8 per cent of the operators and 71.0 per cent of the unemployed were regularly reading the *Sunday Post*. The numbers involved in these movements are, however, small, giving these moves no statistical significance, at best merely hinting at an emerging trend. Figure 10.1 depicts the final readership pattern of selected Sunday papers.

The conclusion here must be that newspaper readership patterns provide us at best with a weak measure of social class affiliation and social mobility when 'social classes' C, D and E are being compared. In so far as one can tell anything from figures, the trainees at the end of the project period were placed on newspaper readership somewhere between the craftsmen on the

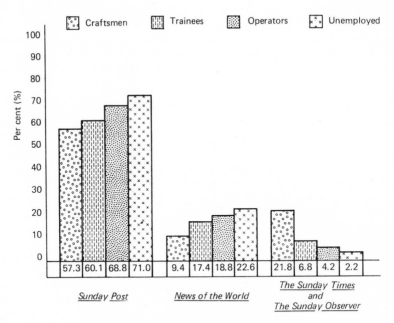

FIG. 10.1   *Sunday newspaper readership*

one hand and the operators and unemployed on the other. This appears
to be in keeping with ownership patterns of household durables and the
like.

TABLE 10.13   *Daily newspaper readership* (%)

| | Trainees | | Crafts-men | Appren-tices | Operators | | Unemployed | |
	Initial	Final	Final	Final	Initial	Final	Initial	Final
Daily Express	50.4	48.4	55.2	46.0	55.2	54.2	58.1	54.8
Daily Record	42.4	38.0	21.9	43.0	38.5	35.4	40.9	43.0
Daily Mail	5.8	2.7	8.3	2.0	4.2	5.2	2.2	1.1
Daily Mirror	4.7	4.7	1.0	5.0	3.1	4.2	2.2	—
Daily Sketch	0.8	—	—	1.0	—	—	—	—
Sun	0.8	1.2	1.0	—	—	1.0	—	—
The Times	0.4	—	2.1	—	—	—	—	—
Anything	0.8	1.2	—	1.0	—	—	—	1.1
Other	—	1.6	4.2	1.0	1.0	1.0	—	1.1
TOTAL N =	258	258	96	100	96	96	93	93

TABLE 10.14   *Sunday newspaper readership* (%)

| | Trainees | | Crafts-men | Appren-tices | Operators | | Unemployed | |
	Initial	Final	Final	Final	Initial	Final	Initial	Final
Sunday Post	65.6	60.1	57.3	68.0	69.8	68.8	76.3	71.0
Sunday Mail	38.0	39.1	35.4	40.0	51.0	44.8	46.2	41.9
News of the								
World	17.1	17.8	9.4	16.0	8.3	18.8	14.0	22.6
The People	16.7	12.4	10.4	12.0	17.7	11.5	14.0	18.3
Sunday Express	13.2	13.2	14.6	12.0	12.5	14.6	12.9	8.6
The Sunday								
Times	3.9	5.0	13.5	5.0	2.1	2.1	1.1	2.2
Sunday Mirror	3.9	8.5	6.3	3.0	3.1	4.2	2.2	—
The Sunday								
Observer	2.7	1.6	7.3	1.0	2.1	2.1	—	—
Anything	1.6	0.4	—	—	—	—	1.1	—
Other	0.4	0.4	1.0	1.0	1.0	1.0	—	1.1
TOTAL N =	258	258	96	100	96	96	93	93

SOCIAL MOBILITY: CONCLUSION

There was a tendency for some members of all of the 'working-class' groups of the research to deny the importance of class in contemporary society; given that British society is certainly more open than it was, say, fifty years ago, such sentiments may make sense. Yet when one considers that few of the interviewees were unwilling to name determinants of 'social class' and very few were thereafter unwilling to rate themselves in the social class structure, the tendency to deny the importance of social class in contemporary Britain by many who did so cannot be taken at face value. Indeed, it would appear reasonable to assume that social class is still significant and that manual workers from a variety of status groups are still well aware of this fact.

At the commencement of the research period no significant difference in the subjective self-rating of the trainees, operators and unemployed was discerned. By the end of the period, however, the trainees rated themselves significantly higher than did the operators and unemployed, yet their self-rating was not as high as that of the craftsmen and of the ex-apprentices. Hence the trainees once again occupied an intermediary position indicating a movement in an upward direction, which success and time are likely to complete.

The ownership of household durables and the like would appear to provide us with one objective measure of social class. Some social mobility was here observed in so far as the trainees at the end of the project period indicated ownership patterns which were higher than those shown by the operators and the unemployed control groups; yet the trainees had not attained the level of the craftsmen. And the ownership pattern observable for the trainees at the end of the research already existed at the beginning, suggesting that the trainees were to a large extent by these criteria a self-selected sample.

Housing was not a good objective indicator of social class or of social mobility. This was assumed to be due to the imbalance in the Scottish housing position with its low owner-occupancy and high rate of local authority housing. When one considers desired housing, a subjective aspect, the aspiration of all groups had risen, which may indicate a measure of upward social mobility for all, but more likely reflects the greatly rising cost of renting a council house. Under the circumstances, desired housing is at best a weak indicator of upward social mobility of the trainees.

Assessment of social mobility on the basis of newspaper readership patterns is fraught with difficulties; it has therefore to be accepted that this provides us with no more than a very weak indicator of social mobility when our interests lie with such mobility within the field of manual workers. The trainees do, however, appear to have once more attained a position above the operators and unemployed but not yet on a level with the craftsmen.

In total it would therefore appear that the trainees, some eighteen months after the completion of their training period, occupied an intermediary position between the craftsmen on the one hand and the operators and the unemployed on the other.

It was observed that those trainees who claimed upward social mobility also tended to be significantly above average in using their training skill, thus association between 'always' using training skills and claiming to have experienced upward social mobility was statistically highly significant. This is hardly surprising, for those trainees who had always throughout the eighteen months of the survey period used their training skill were more likely to view themselves as being successful. A consequence of this is the likely perception of having experienced upward social mobility. It may therefore be hypothesised that in a few years' time, given a further successful employment history, the successful trainees will have caught up with the craftsmen, and in so doing will have left the operators and unemployed behind in the social structure on the basis of both subjective and objective status criteria.

PART III

THE LONG-TERM PERSPECTIVE OF TRAINING THE MATURE WORKER

Chapter 11

The Second Survey: The Trainees' Situation in the Labour Market Half a Decade or More after Entry

INTRODUCTION

The data available from the eighteen-month survey described in the fore-going provided some answers to a variety of questions as, for example, why men attend government training centres, their success in fulfilling the ambitions with which they enter training and the numbers who succeed in making a career in their new trades despite hazards such as lack of experience and possible antagonism from the various groups with whom they come into contact in the post-training industrial environment. However, the results of that research project raised nearly as many questions as it answered. Were the results obtained in this work a phenomenon of the period under study? Would the 177 men (68.8 per cent of the 258 men in the sample) who had always been able to make use of their trades in employment become securely established in these trades or would more men abandon their training and move on to other jobs? The obvious solution to the latter question would have been to prolong the study to examine 'drop-out' rates. Unfortunately this continual contacting of the sample would have become a costly exercise as well as a difficult one because the men in this sample were originally given to believe that their co-operation would be required for only eighteen months following the end of their training. The alternative would have been to contact a group who had been through these post-training experiences and who had left government training centres several years before. That this method was possible was known from the Government Social Survey of 1969 which had contacted men who had attended training centres in 1965 and 1966.[1] Although our English control group had clearly indicated that in the main the experience of our Scottish trainees had not been unique to Scotland, the number of men from Scotland in the Social Survey's national sample was too small to provide any basis for really accurate comparison with the research which has been discussed above. As a result it was decided to contact men who attended

[1] *See Post-Training Careers of Government Training Centre Trainees* (HMSO, 1972).

Dunfermline Government Training Centre in 1964 and 1965 – the only centre at that time in east Scotland. These were the first two years of government training centre activity after the reorganisations brought about by the Industrial Training Act of 1964. Two hundred and forty-nine men were trained in that period and, as may be seen from Table 11.1, 181 men returned completed questionnaires.

TABLE 11.1   *Distribution of sample according to year in which they trained*

	1964	1965	Total
Numbers trained	121	128	249
Refused to help	12	16	28
Could not be traced	11	6	17
Deceased	2	1	3
Numbers available	96	105	201
Withdrew after contact .	5	6	11
No reply	7	2	9
Completed questionnaires	84	97	181

The methods described in Chapter 4 were followed again. A postal questionnaire was sent out, followed by two reminders sent at fortnighty intervals, to those who failed to reply. Finally interviewers visited the non-respondents to help them with the completion of the forms. The time lapse between the last contact with the men when they left the government training centre in 1964 or 1965 and the fieldwork some six or so years later made it difficult to trace some men. Also, direct contact with the trainees could not be made until the Department of Employment had been able to obtain a statement from the trainee of his willingness to help – obviously the Department of Employment is bound by the rules of confidentiality for those who pass through training centres.

The information given by the 181 men who finally completed questionnaires gives the following description of this group. As all had been trained at Dunfermline Government Training Centre their homes tended to be in the east of Scotland; only 12 men (6.6 per cent) came from outside that area. Most men (144 – 79.6 per cent) came from Fife and the Lothians, and the remaining 25 from Angus or farther north on the east coast. The age distribution of the group differed slightly from that of the later group described in the foregoing chapters.[2] None of the trainees was under twenty years of age. As apprenticeships were not completed until twenty-one at that time this was an obvious precaution to avoid confronting craft traditions. A fairly similar proportion of this sample (43.1 per cent compared with 46.5 per cent of the 1968–9 group) was in the 21–30 age group, but

[2] It is now intended to call those trainees included in the longitudinal survey who trained in 1968–9 'sample number one' (or 'first sample') and those who were trained in 1964–5 and are described in this chapter as 'sample number two' (or 'second sample'). ⸢

there were more (38.1 per cent compared with 23.6 per cent) in the 31–40 age group. Only 34 men (18.8 per cent) were aged over 40 compared with 60 men (23.3 per cent) of 'sample number one'. Perhaps as a result of these men being on average older than members of 'first sample' 89.0 per cent were married compared with only 76.0 per cent of the group studied earlier.

PRIOR EDUCATION, TRAINING AND EMPLOYMENT

The education level of the men trained in 1964 and 1965 (sample number two) was higher than that of the men trained later. Seventy-seven men (42.5 per cent) had followed some kind of further education after leaving school compared with only 65 (25.2 per cent) of the first sample. More notably, 17 of the 34 men (50.0 per cent) who were over 40 years of age had attended courses, which compares with only 10.0 per cent of the 60 men in that age-group in the first sample. Further education must often have been related to craft-training, as 54.8 per cent of the 62 men who had enjoyed some sort of craft-training had attended classes compared with 36.4 per cent of the men with no craft-training. Fifteen men had completed apprenticeships earlier in their careers and 47 men had begun apprenticeships but had not completed them. The remaining 118 men had not had any craft-training: 31.4 per cent of the 118 because they were unable to find a training position, 30.5 per cent because of financial reasons, whilst other men appeared to have suffered from a lack of guidance as 11.0 per cent had been influenced by their families to take up other employment and 12.7 per cent were just not interested in having an apprenticed trade. Financial reasons were also a main factor in men giving up apprenticeship training; 15 of the 47 men (31.9 per cent) gave this reason and another 15 said that they stopped training when they joined the Forces. It was good to see that 16 of the 47 men who had abandoned their trades took them up again when they went to the government training centre in addition to another 7 men who attended training allied to their previous trades. This was a higher proportion than the 8 from the 38 men who had done partial apprenticeship training who returned to their trades when training in 1968 or 1969 (the first sample).

It appeared that many men regarded apprenticeship training as leading to the only type of 'skilled' work. Men were asked to grade their previous employment against the scale of skilled, semi-skilled or unskilled. The men's ratings were compared with the official rating given to each job by the Registrar General's Classification of Occupations.[3] Ninety-six men had been in jobs officially classed as skilled but only 37 of these men regarded them as such. And, 44 men felt that their previous employment had been unskilled but the Registrar General's Classification rated only 19 of these jobs as unskilled. This suggests a measure of deliberate downgrading of jobs which trainees held prior to attending government training centres, although it could equally well suggest that the Registrar General's

[3] *Classification of Occupations* (HMSO, 1966).

Classification does not correspond with that of the culture of manual workers at large. Additionally, the men may also have considered these as inferior to jobs which they might hold after training was completed.

However, few men claimed to have attended training because they were dissatisfied with their previous jobs; only 30 men (16.6 per cent) had been dissatisfied or had felt that their jobs offered no prospects. Fifty-five men (30.4 per cent) entered training because they had been made redundant or because they had been ill.[4] Other men, 37 altogether (20.5 per cent), made no claim to having been made redundant but nonetheless their jobs had come to an end for some reason, and only 31 men (17.1 per cent) had left their jobs in order to attend the training centre; these jobs had for a significant number been of a temporary nature while they waited for admittance to a course. Those men who had been forced into training by redundancy or ill-health tended to have been in these jobs for several years and were often in the older age group. Fewer men left regular employment to attend the government training centre than those from the 1968–9 (first) sample. Only 61 men (33.7 per cent) of the second sample were in regular work prior to training compared with 152 men (58.9 per cent) in sample number one. This difference may well be the result of the new image of the government training centres, for in 1964 the training centres were only beginning to train able-bodied men once more after the period of the fifties when they had fulfilled a mainly rehabilitatory function in dealing with men who had been ill, men who had been demobbed from the armed forces, and men who had been unemployed. In 1964 there was still a high proportion in these three categories, in so far as 20 men (11.0 per cent) had been ill, 25 (13.8 per cent) had come from the Forces, and a higher number, 52 (28.7 per cent), had been without work in addition to those 20 men (11.0 per cent) who had been made redundant. This compares with a total of 129 men (50.0 per cent) in the three categories in the 1968–9 (first) sample. The smaller proportion of men in these categories in this later (i.e. 'first') sample may reflect how the government training centres had built up an image of an efficient training organisation instead of being regarded in the main as a refuge for 'old crocks'. One other difference that had occurred in the four years which separated the two samples was that fewer men in the earlier group considered themselves as training after redundancy; only 20 of the 117 men (17.1 per cent) who had been unemployed when applying for training considered themselves 'redundant', but 32 (30.2 per cent) of the 106 unemployed men in the 1968–9 (first) sample had been made redundant. This probably reflects the changes brought about by the 1965 Redundancy Payments Act which conferred the euphemism of redundancy on many normal dismissal procedures.

[4] It will be remembered that in describing the motivating factors for seeking training when discussing the first sample it was suggested that redundancy and illness are less voluntary and less positive reasons for taking up training than were most other motivators. This conclusion is obviously pertinent here, and if it applied to the first sample it must equally apply to this second sample.

The men who had been in regular employment when applying for training were more often in jobs which the Registrar General's Classification would rate as unskilled than were the rest of this second sample. Of the men who were employed when applying for training, 42.9 per cent had been in skilled jobs (this figure is not available for the men in the 1968–9 (first) sample but 43.8 per cent of the total first sample had been in skilled jobs prior to commencing training). Other evidence that men felt their previous employment to be of a low status was evident in the reasons they gave for training. The most often quoted reason was 'to obtain a higher skill'.[5] Twenty-three (37.7 per cent) of the 61 men who left regular work gave this as their most important reason and a further 22 mentioned it as a factor which had influenced their decision to train. Men who came from situations other than regular work also placed importance on this reason (see Table 11.2). In the survey of the men who trained in 1968–9 (first sample) the participants were not asked directly if a search for a higher skill was important, but 10.0 per cent of the men interviewed had mentioned it spontaneously. Direct comparisons here between the two groups are therefore not possible, but the search for skill can be taken as being of importance to some of the latter group also. In the first sample it was found that men who had obtained some experience of the craft system in earlier employment did not place so much emphasis on the desire for a skill as men who had been denied apprenticeship training when young; this was found to be the case again. Less than half of the 62 men who had completed apprenticeships or had partial apprenticeship training wanted a higher skill compared with 56.8 per cent of the 118 men who had no direct experience of craft training.

THE PROBLEM OF SECURITY

In the 1968–9 survey (first sample) the men placed a lot of emphasis on training in order to give them 'security'; 79.8 per cent of the 258 trainees mentioned that training would lead to more security and 113 men gave this as the most important factor influencing their decision to attend a government training centre. It was difficult to establish exactly what the trainees meant by the term 'security' and the positioning of that factor at the head of the list was questioned as a factor in contributing to the high

[5] 'To obtain a higher skill' was also the most often quoted reason for training given by the Social Survey sample (see *Post-Training Careers of Government Training Centres*, op. cit.). The first (1968–9) sample was not given this choice on the original questionnaire, but could of course write it in if they wished – few did so. It was felt when the original questionnaire for sample number one was designed that to give the option 'to obtain a higher skill' would prevent respondents from thinking of the 'real' reason (i.e. is obtaining a skill an end in itself or is it a means towards some other end as for example security or higher status?). When the second sample were given the pre-printed option the largest single number took advantage of it; we still do not know for certain whether obtaining a skill is a good enough reason in itself for seeking training for the majority who gave it as the main motivation for going into training.

rating it was given. In the second survey 'security' was placed sixth in a list of factors, but ranked fourth in the men's selection of factors, as Table 11.2 shows. Higher wages and better job prospects were judged to be more important than security but these factors could possibly be synonymous for some trainees with security (see Chapter 6 pp. 78–82).[6] Other reasons can be more easily explained. Half of the 20 men who left previous employment due to illness quoted ill-health as a reason for attending a government

TABLE 11.2   *Choices made by men of factors influencing their decision to attend training compared with their situation prior to training*

Choices \ Original situation	After illness	After redundancy	Demob.	Unem- ployed	In regular job	Others	Total
Regular work	3	8	5	17	16	—	49 *27.2*
Higher wages	5	9	12	18	45	1	90 *50.0*
Better job prospects	10	12	11	25	36	—	94 *52.2*
Able to move	—	—	1	2	4	—	7 *3.9*
To avoid moving	4	3	—	5	2	—	14 *7.8*
More security	7	7	10	19	36	1	80 *44.4*
Family reasons	1	2	—	1	4	—	8 *4.4*
Health reasons	10	—	—	3	9	—	22 *12.2*
Employment exchange suggestions	9	5	5	19	2	1	41 *22.8*
Wanted a change	2	1	—	12	9	—	24 *13.3*
Obtain a higher skill	6	13	13	20	45	1	98 *54.4*
Other reasons	—	1	3	2	7	—	13 *7.2*
N =	20	20	25	52	61	2	180

Note: Throughout the chapter figures in italics in the tables indicate percentages.

[6] 'Security' may well be a generic term for a variety of hoped-for results. This was not investigated in any depth and must await the outcome of other research; it cannot be usefully discussed further here.

training centre and 9 of these men also spoke of the influence which the employment exchanges had exerted. The influence of the employment exchanges was also evident among the men who had been unemployed and who would have had close contact with the staff of those offices.

Despite some differences in the pre-training background of the two samples, the post-training experiences of the men who trained in 1964–5 (second sample) confirmed many of the hypotheses formed after analyses of the data obtained from the men trained in 1968–9 (first sample). Firstly, the men who experienced unemployment between completion of training and beginning a job were less likely to find skilled work than men who escaped unemployment. For example, 80.5 per cent of the 169 who made full or partial use of their skill in their first jobs had no unemployment, whereas 6 of the 12 men who made no use of their skill in their first jobs had experienced some unemployment. Most unemployment lasted less than six weeks but 10 men took longer than six weeks to find work and only 5 of these managed to find jobs using their trade. This compares with only 7 of the 171 men who had no, or little, unemployment and made no use of their training in their first job.

THE PLACEMENT AND EMPLOYMENT OF THE TRAINEES

The geographical area from which the second sample was drawn was not so widespread as that of the first sample, so differences in employment success were not so varied. What did emerge was that all the men from the north-east of Scotland (the area farthest from the centre) did get skilled jobs eventually but had to experience more unemployment initially than men from other areas. This may reflect the difficulties which government training centre placement officers have in finding jobs outside their immediate area. In 1968–9 trainees from the north-east suffered no more unemployment than trainees from other areas but they did not always find jobs in the north-east and had to move elsewhere. Placement officers did not play as significant a role in job-seeking as they might have done. Only 65 of the second sample (35.9 per cent) claimed that they were found suitable jobs through this government training centre service, and a further 29 men (16.0 per cent) found work with the aid of the employment exchanges. All the others relied on their own efforts. Sixty-one men got jobs after they had visited the premises of the employing organisation, 5 more obtained employment after they had written to the companies, and 6 men gained work by answering newspaper advertisements. Personal contact seemed to play a part; 11 men got their jobs by friends putting in a good word for them with their employers and one man returned to his former employer but with new employment status.

Information on all jobs held by each man since leaving the centre and his opportunities to use his new skill was obtained. From this information it appears that 98 men (54.1 per cent) of this second sample had used their skill in every job since leaving the government training centre and so might be regarded as well established in their new trades. At the other end of the spectrum were 9 men who had never used their training so the period which they spent at the government training centre must be considered a waste of time. Seventy-four men (40.9 per cent) had used their trade in some jobs but not in others. The most usual pattern for men in this last group was to make use of their skill in their first jobs but not in subsequent ones. This pattern is shown in Table 11.3 which illustrates that the drop-out rate is most rapid during the first year after training. If a man can complete the first period successfully then his chances of leaving the trade are reduced. This confirms the experience of the 1968–9 survey, the longer study period, however, indicating the pattern more clearly. Only 3 men reversed the typical pattern; these men, after a bad start, found work in their trades and on the survey date were still making use of their training. This latter job movement is more difficult to accomplish as the trainee may quickly forget the intensive training which he has received when he is not making use of the new information in employment. Additionally, having found a job, he might then be reluctant to move again. Twelve men did not conform to either of these patterns, oscillating in and out of skilled work instead. The reasons behind this are not known, but these men did seem to have a history of short-term jobs and were possibly unwilling or unable to stick to anything.

In this second sample of trainees it was men aged over 40 who were most successful, unlike the 1968–9 group. Twenty of the 34 men (58.8 per cent) aged over 40 always used their skill compared with 78 of the 147 younger man (53.1 per cent). In the other sample, the older men were significantly less successful than the others; at the end of eighteen months only 30 men (50.0 per cent) of the 60 men over 40 were still using their skill compared with 147 (74.2 per cent) of the 198 men under 40. This contradiction in the success of the over-40s in the two samples was partly explained by a spokesman from the Department of Employment who felt that in 1964 the selection of older men was tightly controlled but was later relaxed. This careful selection results in a group of men who appear to have good work records and comparatively high educational achievements.

Men who trained in construction trades were more successful in using their skills than men who trained in some other trades. As in the first sample, agricultural fitters were not successful over the study period although all but one had started in jobs using their training.

Once again it was men in C group (men who never used their trade in employment) who experienced most initial unemployment. Most intermediate unemployment was suffered by men in B group (men who used their training in some jobs but not in others). Given this situation, experience of unemployment must be considered as an active factor in a man's decision to leave his trade. Unemployment prior to training also seems to play an important part. Only 42.3 per cent of the 52 men who were unemployed when they applied to the government training centre were successful in using their skill in every job, which compares badly with the 68.9 per cent of the 61 men who had previously been in regular work and who used their training in every job. Once again the finding is similar to the situation in the other survey. One other fact which points to the importance of the pre-training situation on post-training success is that none of the men who made no use of their skill had been in regular work prior to retraining. This reinforces the conclusion reached on this point when the first survey's findings were discussed.

TABLE 11.3   *Period before leaving trade among trainees who only used their skill sometimes*

Period of time between leaving GTC and abandoning trade	No. of trainees	Cumulative percentages
Under 3 months	4	4
	7.1	7.1
2–6 months	11	15
	19.6	26.8
7–12 months	11	26
	19.6	46.4
Nos. leaving in first year	26	
	46.4	
13–18 months	7	33
	12.5	58.9
19–24 months	7	40
	12.5	71.4
Nos. leaving in second year	14	
	25.0	
Nos. leaving in third year	8	48
	14.3	85.7
Nos. leaving after more than 3 years	8	56
	14.3	100.0
Total left trade N = 56		
Alternated between using and not using trade	12	
Established in trade after bad start	3	
Not clear/don't know	3	
Total in group B	74	

The crucial statistics, however, are not so much those which cover un-employment as those which show which men were still using their training trade at the end of the survey period. As previously stated, 98 men (54.1 per cent) of this sample had used their skill in every job held since leaving the government training centre; and a note of optimism is provided by the fact that a total of 109 men (60.2 per cent) were using their skill in the current job on the survey date or their last job if unemployed on the date of returning the questionnaire (this latter situation applied to only 3 of the 109 men). Put another way, 106 out of 181 men (58.6 per cent) were fully employed in skilled jobs on the survey date. Thus the drift out of skilled jobs over time, as discerned in the 1968–9 (first) sample, appears not to continue much beyond the eighteen-month period and, further, it appears all but arrested and possibly even partially reversed after a post-training period of five years or more.

It was attempted to link earnings levels to success in using the training trade. This was a difficult exercise as the data were obtained over an eigh-teen-month period, covering the first quarter of 1970 to the middle of 1971, and so varied according to the inflationary wage rises of that period. Com-paring earnings of all trainees with those of craftsmen would have been a meaningless exercise – on the basis that like should be compared with like, only successful trainees (i.e. those who had used their training trade throughout) were used for comparison purposes here. The average wages for 'successful' trainees were thus compared with the average wages for craftsmen during 1970 and it was found that although gross wages for successful trainees and for craftsmen were similar, basic wages were lower for trainees. In general, the trainees seemed to make up their lower basic rate with more overtime working.

DIFFICULTIES ENCOUNTERED

Success in becoming established with work-mates, union, and employer was seen to be a complex issue from the work done with the first sample and so was studied further with this second group. Trainees were requested to state if they had experienced any difficulties from employers, time-served men, semi-skilled men, unskilled men, or 'trade unions', and were asked to give details of these difficulties if they could. The comments which were made may have been distorted due to the time factor and are certainly not so accurate as the comments from men in the 1968–9 sample who were reporting on their experiences soon after the events had occurred. Despite this caution, the 1964–5 (second) sample showed again that it was the men who had made some use of their skill but who had been unable to use it with total success who provided most comments. Few difficulties were, as should be expected, attributed to either semi-skilled or unskilled men. The main difficulties encountered were with time-served men; 49 (50.0 per cent) of the 98 men in group A, 43 (58.1 per cent) of the 74 men in group B and 3 (33.3 per cent) of the 9 men in group C all found problems here. Thirty-nine (41.1 per cent) of these 95 men did not elaborate on what form the resistance took but 31 men classed it as straightforward resentment. Eleven men found that they faced the old argument of 'I had to serve five years in my trade, why should you get away with six months?' and 4 others had similar arguments to listen to on the belief that apprenticeship training is the only way of assimilating the 'mysteries' of the craft. In 5 cases craftsmen had actually opposed the employment of a 'trainee' by holding union meetings and threatening strike action if the 'trainees' were employed.

Compared with the 95 trainees who commented on the behaviour of time-served men, only 46 mentioned resistance from employers. Again, most (54.3 per cent) of these men did not elaborate on what type of resistance they met. Exploitation was claimed by 9 men (19.6 per cent) who said they were used for cheap labour. Three employers, it appears, did not want to employ trainees, another four mistrusted and doubted the trainees' abilities whilst two others seemed to expect too much of the men.

Difficulties from unions were also mentioned by 46 men but only 20 of these gave details of such difficulties, the most common of which was that of obtaining union membership; 10 men had experienced this. At least some of this 'trade union' resistance must have been from work-mates acting through official and unofficial trade union channels – and it can therefore be assumed that resistance by work-mates (acting directly to make their resentment felt or indirectly through their trade union) was more often perceived than bona-fide trade union resistance. Although it is difficult to draw any concrete conclusions it would seem that the trade union hierarchy is not, in general, leading resistance to dilution as a means of control, but at times merely carrying out the membership's will and not infrequently leaving it to members as work-mates to make their own resistance felt.

Unlike the 1968–9 group, in this second sample it was the younger men who were the most vocal in their complaints. In the second sample, trained in 1964 and 1965, 60.3 per cent of the 78 men aged under 30 mentioned resistance compared with 46.6 per cent of the 103 trainees older than 30. This may be the result of the young men in their 20s meeting up with their contemporaries who, having fairly recently taken the longer traditional way to a trade, feel that the trainees have cheated in taking a short cut.

Despite the comments, 66 of the 98 men who had been successful in using their skill all the time had joined unions appropriate to their trades. In most cases these men were graded as 'skilled' by the union, but, in the case of the (now) AUEW only 19 of the 26 members were graded as skilled even though they were holding skilled jobs. The remaining 7 men were ranked as semi-skilled or 'dilutee'. This lack of acceptance as skilled men may be a contributory factor in a man's ability to use his training. Thus in group A there were only 15 centre-lathe turners from a group of 27 men who trained in this trade, only 8 of these men being union members and a mere 4 having obtained recognition as fully skilled men.

This resistance from 'unions', employers and employees was seen to have an effect on the trainees' abilities to get the most from their training. In answer to the question 'Have you done as well as you thought you would when you began your training?' almost a third (32.6 per cent) of the 181 men felt that they had not done as well as they would have hoped. A variety of reasons were given for this failure but the most common one was 'hard for the system to accept trainees'. Twelve men felt that there was no obvious role for them and their attempts to find a niche in the work-force had met with resistance. The 7 men who had not done as well as they expected because they could not make use of their training may also have had the difficulty of finding a place in the working community uppermost in their minds.

GEOGRAPHICAL MOBILITY

One of the Department of Employment's criteria for acceptance to a course of training is the man's stated willingness to move home. In the 1968–9 survey a small number of men did move home but these men were no more successful in making use of their training than others, as has already been demonstrated. The same situation was observed from the data obtained from the men trained in 1964 and 1965. Of the 181 men studied, 35 men made moves to locations more than 25 miles away from their previous homes. Only 15 of these men (42.9 per cent) were classed in group A (men using their trade in every job) compared with 83 of the 146 men who did not move, or 56.9 per cent. This difference is not statistically significant but reinforces the findings based on the first survey showing that mobility is no aid to success. Yet paradoxically the reasons for moving were usually related to job problems: 11 men claimed that they had to move because of 'job difficulties'; 12 men to take up a new job; and 10 men to look for work. Personal reasons given were as follows: 6 men gave hunting for a better house; 7 men claimed family reasons; 2 quoted moving to a nicer town; and 10 men gave a variety of other reasons. Thus personal reasons were quoted less often than those related to job problems.

Another point of interest is the faster drop-out rate observed among the mobile men who abandoned their trade. Of the 17 mobile men who left jobs where they were using their training, 12, or 70.6 per cent, did so within the first year compared with 35.9 per cent of the 39 immobile men who left their trades. The background of these mobile men gives a clue to the reasons behind this quick drop-out. Of these men who dropped out, only 1 of the 17 had been in regular employment before training compared with 10 of the 39 immobile men who had dropped out. The mobile men had also shown greater geographical mobility prior to training so it may be that this group was not, in terms of geographical mobility, as stable as others; 21 of the 35 men had moved at least once before compared with 31 of the 132 immobile men.

As in the first sample, men who had to move home or who had to live away from home in order to attend the government training centre were found in disproportionately large numbers among those who moved after training. Fourteen (37.8 per cent) of these 37 men moved compared with 21 (14.6 per cent) of the 144 men who lived in the Lothians or Fife, within daily travelling distance of the centre. This mobility might be the result of tradition or might be due to the fact that a man who is willing to live away during a training course is potentially mobile. What is certain is that this mobility does not relate to the employment situation of the areas. Unemployment statistics from 1964 until 1970 show that east and west Fife (i.e. close to the government training centre attended) had the higher rates when compared with the unemployment figures for Edinburgh, Dundee and Aberdeen areas from which the other trainees generally came.

As in the shorter period first survey, younger men were somewhat more mobile than older trainees; 17 of the 78 men aged under 30 (21.8 per cent) moved, compared with 18 of the 103 older men (17.5 per cent). As well as reasons for mobility, reasons for immobility were asked for, and men who had seriously considered moving yet had not moved were asked what had prevented them from leaving their present home. Forty trainees said that they had thought of moving but 17 men (42.5 per cent) stated that their families were not prepared to move and another 6 trainees (15.0 per cent) felt that they themselves could not leave their homes. The willingness of a man's family to move home is obviously vital to a man's ability to be geographically mobile. Fewer mobile trainees (22.9 per cent of the 35 men) than immobile (59.6 per cent of 146 men) lived within 25 miles of their parents.

CONCLUSION

The work of the second survey, so briefly summarised in this chapter, did not reveal any startling discoveries regarding the fate of men from government training centres five or more years after their training. Rather, it confirmed and amplified some of the findings of the earlier eighteen-month study of men trained in 1968-9 and gives some pointers to the effective use of training centres.

One area in which this work contradicted the earlier research was where it showed that older men need not necessarily always prove unsuccessful following training; men aged over 40 in the second sample, in fact, formed the group most successful in making the most of their training. This is very different from the first 1968-9 sample when age appeared to be a barrier to success. It does prove that age is far less important or possibly, within limits, hardly of any importance at all than was at first thought, so long as the man has a good standard of education and a good employment history. Sadly, once again it tended to be those men who came to the training centre after a period of unemployment who were less successful than their compatriots, regardless of age. This suggests that careful selection is of prime importance if government training centres are to provide a good record of successfully training men for new careers.

Examination of the employment prospects for trainees showed that if a trainee does not succeed in using his trade in his first job after training he is very unlikely to make any use of it at all; the importance of placing trainees in suitable employment is therefore once again emphasised. Also, men who were fortunate enough to suffer no unemployment between leaving the government training centre and beginning their first job were more successful in using their training than those who had a period without work. Of those men who successfully obtained jobs in which they made use of their training, a certain number abandoned their trades. As should be expected, the proportion leaving their trade was highest in the first year and fell off over a period of time. It would appear that once a man is in his trade, time in the trade and experience of using his skill reduce his chances of dropping out. The reasons for men leaving their trades are still not clearly known but would appear to be related to difficulties at work based on resentment from time-served men and to a lesser extent due to opposition from employers and 'unions'. The training itself does not seem to be at fault, although one or two criticisms were received from trainees. The main problems seem to lie with the environment into which the trainee is received when he leaves the centre and his anticipation of his post-training experience, and hence are of an industrial relations and sociological nature: industrial relations in so far as real resistance to integration into the 'skilled' labour market is met on the basis of craft tradition or as an example of skilled men or their organising trade union attempting to control part of the working environment; sociological on the basis of the foregoing, but also based on the perception of the work situation by the trainee himself – which takes us back to the 'action frame of reference' with its emphasis on the *perception* of reality as the main motivator for action. This latter point could, for example, explain the differing experience of the older men in the two samples, or the experience of trainees who enter training directly upon voluntarily leaving paid work as opposed to those men who are forced by circumstances to seek training. It would appear that in general the former anticipate success more readily – and consequently find it.

This second survey confirmed that despite the Department of Employment's desire that men should be willing to move home in order to use their training, mobility had no material effect on successful use of training trade. In this sample, geographical mobility might be seen as a disadvantage where it reflected a history of previous mobility in jobs and homes. If one were to speculate on the basis of this second survey, then the older, more stable man might present a better bet for training than the young, highly mobile man, but even such a conclusion might be premature, given the changes which constantly take place within the labour force and within the economy.

This work has given more substance to the recommendations which could be made to the Department of Employment regarding the economic use of government training centres. The most obvious recommendation to be made is that if the Department of Employment wish the centres to train men for skills which they can use they must choose these men carefully to ensure that they are capable of making best use of what was, by the common acceptance of the vast majority of trainees, training of an excellent quality. The conventional wisdom which maintains that adult trainees cannot integrate into the skilled labour market was confounded.

Chapter 12

Review and Conclusion

Courses of accelerated training for adults in the UK have behind them a history of some fifty years or more, yet for almost the whole of this period they have languished at the periphery of industrial activity. For most of this time the training centres had a social and rehabilitatory role; only infrequently have they played an economic role as well. Now, for good or ill, this has changed: under the Training Opportunities Scheme the centres and their counterparts in industry and further education are to become prime suppliers of skilled labour. The sociological and industrial relations implications of such a change, given the structure and function of the institutions which are involved, either directly or indirectly, in the massive retraining effort now under way, need no exaggeration. At least some of the changes can now be pinpointed.

In the long run things ought to become much easier for the adult trainees entering the skilled labour market, as they will then meet more and more 'craftsmen' who have acquired their skills in the same way as the new entrant. Yet, as John Maynard Keynes remarked, in the long run we are all dead. It is the next decade or two which ought to concern us most, and here the picture is nothing like so clear. It would, for example, need a very brave soul to attempt to forecast with any measure of assurance whether the next generation of trainees, the first to graduate under the Training Opportunities Scheme, will, because of their increased numbers, find it easier or harder to obtain and hold suitable employment. Who, in the end, would like to quarrel with economists who emphasise 'the importance of being unimportant' – an advantage which the trainees of this book certainly enjoyed. Yet it may be that as more trainees come on to the labour market their way of obtaining a skill will become the norm and they will find easier paths to full integration. To obtain this change will require a rapid change in a tradition of resistance to skills dilution. This resistance, as we have seen, is nothing like as thorough or complete as many people appeared to believe when we spoke to them regarding this matter; the data given in the book give one cause for optimism here, if one accepts that retraining is a good thing for the various reasons already mentioned.

164

But as was indicated, traditions are not slavishly followed, they often serve a good purpose, and the tradition of craft apprenticeship rested on the sound foundation of control by the craft unions and their modern successors. Thus to change this tradition will require a change in the industrial situation of craftsmen and possibly of much else in industry, for as long as security and relatively high wages depend on bargaining strength alone, it may be difficult to persuade the majority of 'traditional' craftsmen that they should allow a massive influx of 'retrainees' when one of the main bargaining counters of these groups of industrial workers was that their skills were kept in relatively short supply. And it is not merely the industrial reality, but the perception of that reality as indicated by the 'action frame of reference' which matters. If the hope of smooth integration of large numbers of government trainees into work is to be met, then the work experience of skilled workers will have to be rather different in the future, so that they will perceive security of employment being enhanced by the expedient of retraining, and secure, fair wages, being at least less dependent than in the past on maintaining their skill in constantly short supply.

Given our social system, conflict in industry is inevitable, and is usually solved by a system of accommodation via collective bargaining. Thus one may conclude that the problem of dilution like any other industrial problem, is amenable to solution by this method. The 'unitary frame of reference' [1] which claims legitimacy for one side of industry only has to give way to the 'pluralistic frame of reference' with its many legitimate interests and rights. Employers and trade unions as well as the Government are concerned with the problems of solving redundancy, unemployment and underemployment by the method of retraining. It is still too early to assess the success of the Training Opportunities Scheme, but recent industrial history has shown that control by governmental fiat is frequently less than successful and sometimes even counterproductive (this should surprise no one; the story of 'Prohibition' in the USA should have illustrated this point, if such illustration was necessary). The difficulty is to steer a course between the problems of management and those of the affected workers – which indicates that the method of collective bargaining be utilised. If men are to forgo 'restrictive practices' then management may equally be expected to see a reduction in its 'prerogative'. What is patently obvious is that training, like payments systems, is part of industrial relations and can best be handled by similar methods. It is when we are *not* in a 'zero-sum' situation (i.e. one in which one side can only win at the expense of the other), that success is most likely to result. When all sides of industry form a perception of gaining by retraining after collective bargaining has taken place, then success is assured.

For those trainees whose hopes and expectations were so sadly dashed, the foregoing is a story of unmitigated failure. Yet for those of us who are privileged not to be involved in the situation it is one of success, giving

[1] See A. Fox, *Industrial Sociology and Industrial Relations*, Research Paper No. 3 to the Royal Commission on Trade Unions and Employers Association (1967).

some hope that those changes which appear necessary in order to modernise the training of our skilled labour force will come about – the figures are encouraging. Thus 68.8 per cent of the men were, after an eighteen-month period, settled in jobs where they could make use of their training, and data obtained from men who trained in 1964 and 1965 suggest that most men who leave their training trade do so in the first two years following the end of their training. Men who successfully cope in the early months of their post-training period appear to become safely established in their new trades, so that more than 5 years after leaving the centres some 6 out of every 10 men are still actively engaged in practising their skill. This must be viewed, by any standard, as a success, given the raw material on which the centres worked at that time, and the industrial climate then prevalent. As we have seen, the 'failures' were heavily weighted in the direction of those men who anticipated failure, often from the word go. Those men who anticipated success by and large succeeded. One is therefore once again made aware of the simple fact, well known to sociologists and social psychologists, that the perception of reality is often more significant in shaping action than reality itself.

Some men were too old for a labour market which had no mechanism for allowing older men to perfect their new, rudimentary skills, some were unwilling to move to those areas where jobs were available, some were infirm, and not a few suffered from all these impediments and more. To cap it all, the economy during much of the research period marched steadfastly towards a slump with shrinking demands for all types of labour, yet the first requirement of a successful government training effort is an expanding economy with a shortage of those skills which the centres supply. Fortunately, the post-war history has, by and large, been one of skills shortages and as we moved towards the middle of the seventies we saw a return to this state of affairs. Given sensible behaviour by all sectors of the industrial community and not least of all by those who steer the economy, the signs are that things may go well for the next generation of trainees. The significance of a buoyant labour market becomes apparent when one considers the placement figures for government training centre trainees. Thus in 1970 the number of men who completed training courses in Scotland was 1,666 of whom 1,397 were placed in employment by the government training centres; in 1971, in a worsening national employment situation, the number trained fell to 1,455 of whom only 890 were placed in suitable jobs. The situation in England was not dissimilar, and the history of trainee-placement since then has fairly closely followed this pattern. These figures thus indicate that men from government training centres only obtain jobs easily in a favourable labour market. A booming demand for skilled labour is ideal; employers have said (Chapter 9) that they would use government training centre trainees if they had labour shortages when otherwise they would not employ these men.

Obtaining skilled work as soon as possible after completing the training course is a first priority. It was shown that even a brief period of unemployment demoralises many trainees, and most of all those who anticipate failure. It is precisely men such as these who require an early success or two so as to teach them that their anticipations were in error. Especially at risk here are the older men, whose first failure to obtain a suitable skilled job may merely confirm their worst fears, yet these men are then in danger of joining the hard-core unemployed and when this happens the country suffers a treble loss. Men who could be taxpayers then become recipients of public money and their potential skills are lost to the economy.

It has been shown that older people are more painstaking than their younger compatriots, aiming for perfection rather than for speed.[2] Thus the case of the older trainees emphasises one useful change which could be brought about in the government training effort and one which would depend especially on the goodwill of employers. There is a case for lengthening some of the courses, especially those which have a high diagnostic element. More important, however, is the acceptance of the fact that accelerated courses have limitation and that government training centre trainees are best viewed as improvers, requiring a further period of training on-the-job within an industrial firm to complete the learning process.

Trainees who enter the construction industry are viewed as improvers for the first 60 weeks after leaving the centres, obtaining a wage rising from 85 per cent to 100 per cent of the skilled rate over this period, during which employers get a small grant from the Department of Employment. It may be that this is the best solution, especially if this on-the-job training period were supervised in order to make certain that the trainees obtain minimally satisfactory training. It would be most useful if the concept of 'sponsored training' (by which a firm now sends a man to a government training centre for a brief period in order that he may learn a specific skill) were extended so that most trainees 'belonged' to a given firm (and trade union) from the start – the training centre could then guide the man's training in the required direction. We, throughout the research period, were constantly pleasantly surprised by the many ways in which the centre managers and their staffs proved willing to meet the needs of industry. It goes almost without saying that any skill which is barely learnt, disappears rapidly if not then practised, and this is true for younger as well as for the older men, although sadly the older men are again at a greater disadvantage.

Perhaps one worrying aspect of the Training Opportunities Scheme is the implication of 'training for stock', i.e. training during periods of heavy unemployment and making use of these men at a later date, when possibly the economy is on the upswing again. One doubts whether psychologists in the field of learning theory would uphold any such ideas, given the limited training which, due to the short duration of the courses, the centres can offer. And it was demonstrated above that men who were unable to use their training within a short time of leaving their government training centre were unlikely to use their skills at all. Additionally in a depressed

[2] E. Belbin and R. M. Belbin, *Problems of Adult Retraining* (Heinemann, 1972).

economy the 'traditionally-trained' craftsman may also be without work
and would naturally resent the production of more skilled men to compete
for the fewer jobs available. The net outcome of this may be that resentment grows to antagonism and leads to a refusal to accept trainees both
in periods of depression and later. Thus we see once more that training
produces 'problems' and hence can lead to conflict. In a pluralistic society
this is best met by agreement from all sides of industry.

The onus of a successful government training effort therefore depends
on the goodwill of employers and the efficiency of those who steer the
economy. Yet not on those alone, for it was shown that antagonism from
work-mates and unions can be significant in deterring some trainees from
using their new skill. But much of this resistance rests, as we have seen, on
the solid foundation of tradition, and the importance of any tradition is
that it became such precisely because it functioned well in the past. If such
tradition is to change, then it has to be proven to the craftsman and his
representative that such a change is not to his disadvantage. To ask skilled
men to change their attitudes for the good of the community when they
themselves will lose in the process is unreasonable. Nor as we have seen
can the Government legislate so as to change the traditions of the craftsmen – the behaviour of trade unions following upon the introduction of
the Industrial Relations Act being too obviously a case in point here.
Logically the most telling argument, and the one which is most likely to
be listened to, is one appealing to enlightened self-interest. If men, upon
their skill becoming redundant, could be certain of retraining and re-
employment in a new skill this may persuade skilled, time-served men to
support the government training effort. It may not be accidental that a
large proportion of trainees sought security – which is what the established
tradesman hopes already to possess and which he fears to lose if he permits
'dilution'. If one were able to demonstrate that this is not so, one's arguments would be less likely to fall on deaf ears. Inevitably this must mean
that existing craftsmen get priority for training places. Another fact, but
as yet unknown to the craftsman, is that adult trainees who get a first skill
in later life do not get a free 'skilled ticket'; they too 'buy' it by reduced
earnings during the training period. This seemed to be unknown to the
majority of craftsmen, many of whom appeared to think that the trainees
had obtained the best of both worlds – high wages when young and a skill
on the cheap later, when it entailed no sacrifice on the part of the trainees.
Given this ignorance of the sacrifices made by the trainees in order to
undertake training, it is perhaps surprising that resistance was not significantly greater than it was found to be. If these sacrifices were made
known to the skilled men and at the same time was coupled to rising wages
for apprentices, thus making that financial sacrifice less significant, so
much the better. Finally, as has already been discussed, if wage-rates did
not depend to such an extent on the economic forces of supply and demand,
which at this time they so often do, and especially so for craftsmen, then
this may help to open the tradition-guarded doors of craft skills – yet this

last point is so complex as to be well outside the scope of this book, given the post-war history of the various incomes policies. Finally, we noted that it is in the main not at national level, where trade union leaders depend on strength of numbers to support them, but at local level, where an increase in numbers is often seen as a reduction in bargaining strength, that resistance is most likely to arise. But once again, the findings of the research put the emphasis on acceptance rather than on rejection.

In the final analysis, a learning institution is as good as the human material which enters its portals. Whilst there are always exceptions it was the group of trainees who volunteered for training whilst in employment which was most successful in the post-training period. Not a few of these men sought a measure of upward social mobility. This must not be exaggerated, nor should it cause surprise in a stratified society like ours. If, however, we view the post-training situation of the trainees in Lockwood's framework[3] of market, work and status situation, all the foregoing indicates that successful trainees gained on all three dimensions. Once fully integrated in the skilled work-force, they had obtained a greater measure of security – the search for which was frequently the major motivator for entering training; their chances of promotion were enhanced and their wages rose; in general their market situation saw a significant upward swing. The work dimension, too, indicates that the successful trainees gained significantly. Most skilled men have a much larger measure of autonomy at work than do their less skilled colleagues and although we did not set out to obtain information on specific aspects of the work situation of the trainees, sufficient comments were received to make it clear that many trainees perceived a major gain on this dimension. Finally, as Chapter 10 attempts to demonstrate, many trainees not only gained in terms of social status but were clearly aware of this. And even for those to whom such a gain was of little or no consequence, society at large was more likely to give prestige to men practising a high-level manual skill than to those who worked in semi- or unskilled occupations. Naturally, however, it was those who had a clear perception of the status hierarchy of occupations who were most likely to perceive a worthwhile gain on the status dimension.

Given the limited time available for training, the training centres must be viewed as places meriting commendation. One hundred and seventy men from the longitudinal study (65.8 per cent) thought their training either good or very good, and only one in ten of the trainees rated his training as 'poor'. Obviously there is room for improvement, yet on any balanced view one doubts whether many other establishments could easily better such a record.[4] In some respects the centres are their own worst

---

[3] D. Lockwood, *The Blackcoated Worker* (Allen & Unwin, 1958).

[4] It is the intention of the research unit in which the work described here was undertaken to assess the satisfaction of graduates with their 'training' some years after graduating – given that this project is in its infancy no data was available, but few university lecturers, we would think, would be dissatisfied if 90 per cent of their students indicated satisfaction with their course of study.

enemies, for they cannot in a period of six or twelve months train a man to perform his skill, immediately upon finishing his course, at experienced worker standard of speed and quality – an impression which they sometimes seem to project. Unfortunately some of the men and employers seemed to think that this standard should be possible for the raw 'graduate'. This reinforces the case for 'improverships' discussed above.

It will have been noted that some of the trainees interviewed at the beginning of the exercise were not available to us at its conclusion, for they had been removed from their courses (see p. 64). This is worrying, especially since some of them had volunteered whilst in employment – these are in general the most desirable recruits – and were after a three-week probationary period put off the course when their previous job may no longer have been open to them. There is much to be said for a probationary period – few would doubt that the best aptitude tests are those in which the testee is made to perform the actual task in a rudimentary form after suitable introductory instruction. And inevitably there will be a few who do not make the grade. A solution to this problem is a two-tier approach to training, when all entrants are given a limited skills course of, say, six weeks' duration, and the best performers are then put on the full skills course. As an example all entrants to a motor-vehicle course could be taught 'forecourt' skills whilst those able to go on are given a full motor-mechanic's course. In a limited way the above is now being introduced – its extension to all skills is long overdue.

Perhaps it came as no surprise that amongst 'volunteers' for training, who sought training whilst in employment, many did so in order to obtain work which would offer them more job satisfaction, i.e. which improved their 'work' situation. It is a salutary thought, which those of us who are fortunate enough to enjoy interesting work should remember, that many workers are indeed alienated by tedious, routinised work. Whilst for most trainees who succeeded in their post-government training centre career the investment in training seemed to pay off in financial terms, for not a few it was the satisfaction of an interesting job which was most telling. The problems of alienation experienced by many workers in modern manufacture have been a constant theme in modern industrial sociology and it is not our intention to add to either the debate or the massive volume of work done by sociologists on this real problem facing 'industrial man'. Yet time and again one was made aware of the significance of training to many trainees as a means of escaping the tedium which so much of our work-force faces in its workaday life.

For good or ill, then, the government training effort has been radically increased and will continue to be so. Its success is still problematic, yet the signs, as indicated by the research projects described in the foregoing, augur well for the future. Many changes, in attitudes no less than in the mechanisms of training, still need to be accomplished. When all is said and done, however, the successful establishment in skilled trades of the majority of trainees was no mean feat, and the fact that after one or two post-training jobs some trainees were able to hide their government training centre background and many more were able to work equally satisfactorily in an industrial world populated by time-served men, says much for the quality of their instruction no less than for the quality of the men themselves.

The accelerated courses have shown that, given goodwill and adequate industrial experience after leaving the centres, it is possible to teach the required knowledge for a craft-skill in a relatively short period which may point to greatly reduced apprenticeship periods for youth apprentices also. The whole of the industrial community has much to gain and may have little to lose by rethinking its values here providing traditional attitudes can be changed – and this is only likely to come about if it is possible to demonstrate that these traditions no longer serve the purpose for which they came into being. This once again raises the whole problem of control; trade unionists are unlikely to forgo a well-proven machinery for safeguarding their members' market, work and status situations, unless it can be demonstrated beyond doubt over an extended period of time that the change is not to their members' detriment; to do otherwise would be a serious failure of duty to the membership. If apprenticeship periods were reduced it might be possible to pay apprentices significantly more, which in turn would leave just one final step – that of removing age barriers to skills training. One thing is certain; no person now living can forecast the skills requirements over a lifetime. The need for the accelerated courses is therefore self-evident. One could even argue that the very word 'apprentice' should be abandoned and the generic term 'trainee' be used instead for all those who are in the process of acquiring a new skill, no matter at what level of sophistication. Training cannot be viewed as a once-for-all period in one's life, but rather as something which is with us for the whole of our working lifespan.

Subject Index

Author Index

Allen, V. L. 127, 138
Becker, G. 51, 52
Belbin, E. 16, 59, 83, 85, 167
Belbin, R. M. 16, 167
Beynon, H. 16, 23
Brannan, R. 49
Bredemeier, H. C. 128
Brown, R. 49
Burns, T. 18, 66
Centers, R. 80, 130
Clapham, J. H. 32
Clegg, H. A. 27
Clough, G. 28
Cole, G. D. H. 28, 35
Deane, P. 33
Flanders, A. 37, 51, 128
Flinn, M. W. 28, 29, 31
Fox, A. 27, 165
Gerth, H. 126
Giddens, A. 23, 127
Glass, D. V. 126
Goldthorpe, J. H. 18, 24, 29
Grant, I. F. 28
Gresez, J. 63
Hall, J. 126
Hall, K. 80
Hill, C. 29, 31
Hoggart, R. 135
Hughes, J. J. 58
Johnson, P. S. 52
Jones, D. C. 126

Jones, J. A. G. 58
Jones, R. M. 80
Keynes, J. M. 164
Liepmann, K. 27, 38, 48, 57
Lockwood, D. 23, 24, 127, 169
Martin, F. M. 24
Mathias, R. 33, 34
Miller, I. 80
Mitchell, E. 128
Moxham, J. 58
Owen, R. 34
Postgate, R. 35
Rapoport, R. N. 107
Rodgers, A. 49
Rossi, P. H. 108
Runciman, W. G. 129n
Seymour, W. D. 51
Smith, A. 33
Somers, G. 63
Stalker, J. 18
Stephenson, R. M. 128
Thomas, B. 58
Thomson, A. F. 27
Trevelyan, G. M. 29, 30, 31, 34
Unwin, G. 38
Weber, M. 23, 126
Williams, G. 27, 34, 48, 49
Woodward, J. 18
Wright Mills, C. 48
Ziderman, A. 58